Library
2.0

Library 2.0

A GUIDE TO
Participatory Library Service

Michael E. Casey
Laura C. Savastinuk

Information Today, Inc.
Medford, New Jersey

Second printing, 2007

Library 2.0: A Guide to Participatory Library Service

Copyright © 2007 by Michael E. Casey and Laura C. Savastinuk

Library of Congress Cataloging-in-Publication Data

Casey, Michael E., 1967-
  Library 2.0 : a guide to participatory library service / Michael E. Casey. Laura C. Savastinuk.
    p. cm.
  Includes bibliographical references and index.
  ISBN 978-1-57387-297-3
  1. Library planning. 2. Public services (Libraries) 3. Organizational change. 4. Libraries--Information technology. 5. Libraries and the Internet. I. Savastinuk, Laura C., 1979-. II. Title: Library two point zero.
  Z678.C35 2007
  025.1--dc22

                                                                    2007005247

Printed and bound in the United States of America

President and CEO: Thomas H. Hogan, Sr.
Editor-in-Chief and Publisher: John B. Bryans
Managing Editor: Amy M. Reeve
Project Editor: Rachel Singer Gordon
VP Graphics and Production: M. Heide Dengler
Book Designer: Kara Mia Jalkowski
Cover Designer: Shelley Szajner
Copyeditor: Pat Hadley-Miller
Proofreader: Barbara Brynko
Indexer: Sharon Hughes

For our families,

with love and gratitude for their patience and support:

Heather, Sophia, and Holden Casey

Paul Savastinuk

Contents

Chapter 5 Participatory Service and the Long Tail

Figures

Acknowledgments

We wish to thank several people who were instrumental in the development of Library 2.0 and the writing and research for this book, particularly Michael Stephens, Jenny Levine, Stephen Abram, Paul Miller, John Blyberg, Meredith Farkas, Sarah Houghton, Jessamyn West, Walt Crawford, and the many others whose discourse helped to develop the idea of Library 2.0. Without their interest in this concept, both supportive and constructively critical, Library 2.0 would not have evolved to where it is today. We also would like to thank Jo Ann Pinder for sharing with us her vision of the future of libraries and for her notable dedication to the profession; Meg Wilson, for her selfless support, humor, and her incredible insight as a library professional; and Chris Hall, for his intuition and ability to see the many roles that Web 2.0 tools can play in public libraries. We are humbled by our peers, the staff and administrators of Gwinnett County Public Library (GCPL), notably Nancy Stanberry-Kellam, Rhonda Boyd, Donna Pollet, and Lisa Williams, who consistently demonstrate their commitment to the needs of library users. Through their continued dedication to superior customer service, GCPL is well on its way to Library 2.0. We also wish to thank all who participated in the Libraries, Librarians, and Change survey. Their comments, opinions, and suggestions gave us great insight into the effect of change on libraries, library staff, and library users. Finally, we also thank the staff at Information Today, Inc., John Bryans, Amy Reeve, and our editor, Rachel Singer Gordon, for their assistance and guidance throughout this project.

Foreword

On September 23, 2005, Michael Casey uploaded a picture into his Flickr account—a screenshot, actually, of Library Crunch titled "Another Useless Blog." I had subscribed to Michael's Flickr photos a few weeks before, when I'd discovered "Rock the Shelves" in his photostream and asked to use an image of teens enjoying rock music in the library in an "Optimizing Technology in Libraries" presentation. This time, though, something else caught my eye. Library Crunch was another new library blog, yes, but its tagline was what spoke to me: "By a librarian trying to bring forth Library 2.0." I had a definite "aha!" moment.

This was what some library futurists, innovators, and commentators had been talking about for a while: a shift in thinking about libraries. When I scanned the first few entries and read the next few weeks of posts, as Michael's thoughts on building better library services crystallized, I realized we were singing the same tune. His posts echoed many of my talks about technology planning, implementing social tools, creating change in libraries, and librarians optimizing their skills to fulfill the greater mission of libraries.

I need to take Michael to task a bit for describing his blog as "useless." On the contrary, Library Crunch has been thought provoking, insightful, and well written for more than a year now. It also speaks of the power of this little social software tool: Any librarian with something to say can easily add their voices via their own blogs, or through comments at established blogs.

And what of Library 2.0?

In the months since Library Crunch launched, we've seen discussion of the term and the thinking behind it play out across the biblioblogosphere. Some folks had similar "aha!" moments. Others didn't care for the phrase or didn't like attaching a buzzword like "2.0" to the world of libraries. But, no matter where your opinions fell, it certainly was an incredible time to participate in a much-needed discussion—where any librarian could blog or comment and share their views.

What was "born in the biblioblogosphere" has moved beyond the realm of blogs. This has been a fascinating journey. In the drama of the moment, some growing pains at points made it seem like the conversation was disintegrating. Library 2.0 as meme, however, as a way to approach library services, as a way to jumpstart innovation, and as simply the name for a set of principles and philosophies has become firmly planted—not only in the world of library and librarians' blogs, but in our professional literature, conferences, workshops, and associations.

The culmination of this discourse is in your hands. In this book, you'll discover the thinking behind Library 2.0 and its implementation, from user-centered planning to the need for constant evaluation. One of the things I like best about the book is that it discusses the importance of preparing for and dealing with change—a skill every librarian should possess. Michael and Laura Savastinuk present models for creating change in libraries that look forward while never losing sight of our mission, our professional foundations, and the people who have always used libraries. This model is not just for serving Millennials. It's not just for the well-heeled techno-elite. It's a service model for everyone—those who support the library and those who may not have visited a library for many years, if at all.

I feel fortunate that Michael and I have had many opportunities to discuss L2, in person, online, and via the blogosphere. My favorite parts of those discussions have been about the emotional, personal aspects of L2, which include:

Library 2.0 encourages the heart. As we reach out to our users, we remember all of the folks we serve.

Library 2.0 will be a meeting place, either online or in the physical world, where the emotional needs of users will be fulfilled through entertainment, information, and the ability to add their own creations to the Long Tail of content.

Library 2.0 is human. Users will see the face of the library, no matter how they access its services. Librarians will guide them via electronic methods, as well as in person. Versed in the social tools, able to roll with each wave of change, these librarians will encourage and educate future users.

—Michael Stephens

About the Web Page
www.librarychange.com

We hope that the Library 2.0 Web page will serve as a source of supplemental information for the book. We will use it to maintain an updated list of the links that are mentioned in the book, as well as to post additional responses and quotes from the Libraries, Librarians, and Change survey. The page will include a list of blogs that discuss Library 2.0 and will be checked regularly for outdated links. Additional Library 2.0 Web sites of interest, including links to libraries that have made strides toward Library 2.0, will be added as well.

Disclaimer

Introduction

"Libraries need to be able to take reasoned risks to push the envelope when a clear trend emerges and a different way of envisioning and delivering services makes sense."

—Steve Watkins

In August 2005, when Michael Casey first began thinking about the implications of Web 2.0 for libraries, he never imagined that so many others in the library community were wondering the exact same thing. Indeed, librarians around the world were also thinking about how ubiquitous technology and the changing needs of library users would impact library service; all Michael did was give this discussion a name. At this point, Library 2.0 was merely a term without a clear definition. It came with one main question: How can Web 2.0 make libraries better?

Casey launched the first Library 2.0 blog in September 2005, naming it LibraryCrunch (www.librarycrunch.com). Bloggers and librarians from around the world soon joined the discussion on their own blogs, at conferences, and in their libraries. In October 2005, shortly after LibraryCrunch was launched, we received word that Michael Stephens discussed Library 2.0 at the Internet Librarian 2005 conference in Monterey, California. In retrospect, it is unsurprising how quickly this concept developed and was picked up by other librarians. Even before the name was coined, elements of Library 2.0 were already being discussed and debated—well before LibraryCrunch was created. Without the open-minded and constructively critical conversation that occurred over the next year, Library 2.0 may never have been clearly defined. Even though Casey is known for coining the term "Library 2.0," no one person can take responsibility for the evolved definition or the wave of discussion that has made this model so popular and intriguing today.

Web 2.0 and Business 2.0 provided the impetus for the Library 2.0 name and for much of the initial discussion and attempts to clearly define Library 2.0. However large a role technology played in the initial discussion, it soon became clear that the changes libraries need to make to keep up with their users involve much more than just technology. Fortunately for library users, our understanding of what Library 2.0 can do for libraries evolved to include a method of constant change, which includes reevaluating library services and what our users need. Most importantly, Library 2.0 became less about what we can provide to our users and more about what we can allow our users to provide themselves. Participatory service and change are the heart of Library 2.0, and technology is a tool that can help us get there.

We hope this book will help librarians, library administrators, support staff, and students gain a greater understanding of what Library 2.0 is, and how it can be used to revitalize library services for our users. These concepts and ideas are relevant to public, academic, and special libraries. There is no one-size-fits-all model; however, the basic components of Library 2.0 can be applied to just about any library willing and able to take the necessary steps. Because of our public library experience, much of the discussion in this book involves examples from public libraries, although we believe you will still find the content applicable to your organization.

We decided to write this book for the same reason that much of the library community has taken an interest in Library 2.0: We want to improve library service. Every librarian has the goal of offering the best possible service to library users. Library 2.0 can help us achieve and maintain this goal in a rapidly changing environment.

In April 2006, we conducted an online survey about change using the SurveyMonkey Web site (www.surveymonkey.com). Survey questions, statistics, and some responses are provided in Appendix A, and we refer to this survey and its responses several times throughout this book. In this survey, we sought the input of librarians, library staff, and library administrators. We asked questions that would help us gain a greater understanding of how respondents view the effects of change on services, procedures, and other operations within their libraries. Survey respondents had a lot to say about change:

- "Change for the sake of having change is not good enough. There needs to be a direction, target, or goal. The change needs to be measurable and objective—subjective change is OK when it supports the overall goal, but it's a mushy measure."

- "I like many of the changes our administrator has handed down to us to implement, but sometimes feel shut out of the decision process. Many librarians I meet (at conferences) seem way too tradition-bound and seek comfort from each other so that they may remain 'stagnated' yet another year. I hear a lot about how patrons just don't understand."

- "Embracing change can be scary. But once a library starts to change and decides to see change as a constant state, then it becomes easier and easier. Rather like kinetic energy, it is easier to change when you are already moving forward."

- "So much is still 'the way we've always done it.' My supervisor is very supportive of new ideas, but my co-workers, the library lifers, are not."

- "Change is good. However, when you have limited resources you have to be careful how you go about it. You also have to have a high tolerance for failure and the patience to stick with something you know will work until it finds its place."

- "The key is to not stick with the changes that failed. Don't be afraid to say something isn't working and go back to how you used to do it."

- "What is wearing down me and my co-workers is rampant, ill-conceived, unscheduled change with little input from people on the front lines. If change was managed differently, the results would be much better."

- "This is a very exciting time to be working in libraries, and I think that it will be that way for many years to come. At first, I hesitated to go to library school, but as I saw the changes taking place in librarianship, I was convinced that that was where I wanted to be."

Libraries have changed quite a bit over the past couple of decades. In fact, many of the survey responses we received commented on the fact that change itself is already happening; it just isn't always well managed or fails to incorporate the type of change that will best meet our customers' changing needs. Much of this book describes a method for managing change that we and many other librarians would like see libraries adapt—and libraries *must* adapt to keep up with the changing needs of our users. Here's the truth:

- We are losing the interest of our users.

- We no longer consistently offer the services our users want.

- We are resistant to changing services that we consider traditional or fundamental to library service.

- We are no longer the first place many of our current and potential customers look for information.

Given these challenges, how can a library keep its current customers *and* reach potential users who are not already using its services? We hope this book will help you answer this question for your organization.

Chapter 1 explains that there is no one way to get to Library 2.0 that works for all organizations; you must consider both your library's stated mission and your community's needs. Chapter 2 covers the basics of Library 2.0, including an introduction to each of the essential components that will get you there. Chapter 3 explains the importance of knowing your market and competition and providing easy ways to remain aware of your customers' needs and wants. Constant change, a major component of Library 2.0 that is briefly introduced in Chapter 2, is explained in greater detail in Chapter 4, which also includes a method for implementing a system of continual change into your organizational structure. Chapter 5 covers another major component of Library 2.0, user participation, and also discusses the ability for libraries to reach the Long Tail using participatory services and constant change. Chapter 6 provides examples of technologies that libraries can use as tools to reach their Library 2.0 goals. Achieving buy-in from staff, administrators, and the governing board of a library is discussed in Chapter 7. Chapter 8 provides suggestions your organization can use to maintain the momentum for change toward Library 2.0. Chapter 9 covers final considerations about Library 2.0 and the changing needs of library users.

It is our hope that you will use this book to start the process of implementing Library 2.0 changes in your organization. Enjoy!

1

Brand Library 2.0

*"Libraries need to offer traditional services more
efficiently and new services which appeal to those
comfortable with new ways of accessing information."*
                                                —Anonymous

Change is everywhere. Like the steadily increasing processing
power of computers, our lives are growing ever more complex.
Advances in technology allow us to do more with every minute of our
waking day. We can log on and check our e-mail in the morning with
our high-speed, always-on Internet connection; we can use cell phones
to talk to our co-workers and family on the car ride to work; we can
multitask at our desks using our powerful computers; and we can take
our PDAs with us to lunch to let us instantly respond to incoming
e-mail messages. Every minute of our day, we can "be in touch."
Attending our children's after-school events has taken on new meaning, as we see people instantly uploading photos onto their Flickr
account, responding to last-minute queries from their boss, and checking the stock closings, all with their ever smaller handheld devices.
Technology allows us to work, play, and entertain ourselves no matter
where we are—no matter what time of day.

Today we are interacting and communicating on a level unprece-
dented in human history. Thousands of information sources, in print and
on television, radio, and the Internet, bombard our senses. We juggle

1

work and family, with an increasingly blurry line separating the two. Our lives are undergoing constant and often disruptive change, and libraries are along for the ride.

Although libraries have always changed, the pace of that change somehow feels faster now than ever before. We have moved from handwritten manuscripts to low-cost industrial printing, from private or pay libraries to open and free public libraries, from handwritten card catalogs to typed card catalogs to electronic online card catalogs. Libraries have become central to our communities, serving as meeting places and social centers. Change has been constant for libraries. But why does *this* change feel so much faster, so much deeper? This change feels faster because in many ways it *is* faster. Technology has played a key role in this perception of change, but it is by no means the only factor. Shifting population centers, changing demographics, and the cyclical ups and downs of the economic roller coaster all contribute to the change with which libraries must deal.

All around us, we see big-picture changes. Business is learning to operate under new rules. No longer operating in a vacuum, business knows it must live and die by the connected marketplace. Heeding the advice of *The Cluetrain Manifesto*, today's business listens to its customers' conversations. The philosophy behind this is well summed up in this brief quotation:

> A powerful global conversation has begun. Through the Internet, people are discovering and inventing new ways to share relevant knowledge with blinding speed. As a direct result, markets are getting smarter—and getting smarter faster than most companies.[1]

This conversation has resulted in new expectations: expectations for better usability, for faster responses to customer demands, and for an ultimately better product. Business 2.0, as defined by Chris Anderson and James Daly, founders of *Business 2.0* magazine, is about a growing marketplace that demands greater efficiency and value while operating in a world that is less affected by time and space than ever before, due to the growing interconnectivity of the market itself. At the center of Business 2.0 stands the customer, demanding better products and services, expecting excellent customer service, and being secure in the knowledge that they have many choices of places to buy the things they want.

These fundamental changes in the way the business model operates also underlie the development of Web 2.0. Web 2.0, or the "participatory Web," has its roots in simple technologies that allow such collaborative and social Web applications as blogs and wikis to operate as conduits for user participation. These simple tools open up an environment where each user can collaborate with other users and contribute content to other Web sites. This ability to talk and contribute has done nothing less than change the way we interact with businesses.

Complicating these changes is the ever-present dark cloud of politics that has come to play an increasingly heavy hand in contemporary library operations. In the past 10 years, we have seen the USA PATRIOT Act and Children's Internet Protection Act, innumerable censorship challenges, and privacy issues regarding customer records and RFID (Radio Frequency Identification). The ALA's Office for Intellectual Freedom works heroically to defend libraries and the rights of library users, but the battle seems to grow more daunting every year. By the time you hold this book in your hands, will libraries still be able to link to MySpace and Flickr? Only time will tell.

On a local level, libraries face change in the form of increased demand for greater efficiency. Changing staffing levels in libraries have created the need for new ways to operate efficiently. Reductions in staff directly affect staffing models and the ability to deliver quality customer service, and libraries are reaching out to find new tools that allow them to operate more efficiently. RFID, self-check, downloadable audio and video, and the one-desk model all seek to increase the efficiency of the library staff and the self-sufficiency of the customer.

Library systems in areas with growing populations often face the dilemma year after year of providing more services to more people, all while using the same budget figures. The desire to open new branches, expand operating hours, and provide more services in many cases conflicts with the reality of library budgets. Libraries in communities with decreasing populations and tax revenues often find themselves first on the chopping block when it comes to budget cutbacks. Reduced staff, reduced materials budgets, and reduced service budgets can signal the beginning of the end for libraries in economically depressed areas.

These staffing level and model changes hurt more than just the library user; they also hurt library staff. Faced with more work and greater demands, library staff are wilting under the intense pressure and demand for efficiency. Staff members arrive to work ready to dive right into the first task or program of the day, with little downtime available. Whereas staff would once come in and have the time to talk with each other and discuss library issues, today's library staff is a model of greater efficiency. This efficiency is not in itself a bad thing, but its impact on staff must be addressed. The fact that there is less time for staff to talk, share concerns, and discuss issues and recently completed and upcoming events means that staff will communicate with each other less. Unfortunately, a certain level of communication is vital to workplace morale and overall operations. A team of staff members that fails to communicate with each other cannot succeed.

Local change is also reflected in shifting customer expectations. As our user base becomes savvier and more comfortable with the plethora of online electronic resources, we as librarians face increased challenges with regards to getting those people to use library services. Our customers' knowledge is growing. They are far more likely to go to Google or Wikipedia before getting in their cars and driving to the library. But even more telling is the fact that our customers don't first turn to their library's Web site when seeking an answer to their questions. It is not just that there are alternative sources out there; it is also the fact that we are competing with so many other commercial and nonprofit services. Our current and potential users have only a finite amount of time, and we as librarians find ourselves competing against family events, after-school activities, work, bookstores, television, the

Internet, electronic games, and more, in our quest for our customers' attention.

We are fighting for the attention of our users, and, like many businesses, we are losing this battle. The 2005 OCLC (Online Computer Library Center) report *Perceptions of Libraries and Information Resources* (www.oclc.org/reports/2005perceptions.htm) illustrates that libraries are far from the first place people turn when looking for answers. Our community of users is not aware of the services that we offer. Users do not know that we have online databases, for example, so, of course, they do not know what those databases can provide. Our community knows one thing about the library—books. Books are not simply at the top of the list of library brands, books *are* the list.

Change is coming at us from all angles, and we need to be able to respond. We need to listen to those conversations, as *The Cluetrain Manifesto* suggests, and we need to be able to reach out to our users. We *want* to do this. We have always wanted to bring more users into our buildings. We want to continue serving our communities. In fact, we want to serve them with more, with the same budget or less. We want to do it all. The question is, how?

Enter Library 2.0, the idea.

A (BRIEF) DEFINITION

What is Library 2.0? Numerous excellent definitions have been suggested. When thinking and talking about Library 2.0, it is important that any definition include the following:

- Library 2.0 is a model for constant and purposeful change.

- Library 2.0 empowers library users through participatory, user-driven services.

- Through the implementation of the first two elements, Library 2.0 seeks to improve services to current library users while also reaching out to potential library users.

The changes involved in Library 2.0 are specifically designed to improve library services, procedures, and other operations; essentially, Library 2.0 requires the constant evaluation and updating of library services whenever necessary. This change reflects the ever-changing needs of our users. Library 2.0 also empowers library users by giving them the opportunity to assist in the creation and content management of services. This can be accomplished through current and potential user feedback, as well as through the offering of services that rely on active input, such as customer-submitted book reviews or tags that go in the catalog. Finally, Library 2.0 seeks to improve services for current library users, as well as reach the Long Tail of potential users (who are not currently using library services) through the implementation of the first two components. We explain the basics of Library 2.0 in further detail in Chapter 2; the Long Tail as it relates to libraries is further described in Chapter 5.

If you are wondering where technology plays a role in Library 2.0, realize that technology, while an excellent tool that libraries can use to work toward Library 2.0, is not a primary element of this model. It was through rapidly changing technology-based service offerings that librarians initially were able to see the possibilities of reaching Library 2.0, and indeed, you may find that many services your library offers to accomplish Library 2.0 goals involve technology. Still, technology is just a tool that we can use to reach our users. Those libraries that change their operations and ways of thinking to include the fundamental elements of Library 2.0, user empowerment and constant change, will be better able to reach current and potential users than will those who just buy a bunch of new cool toys. A library branch manager told us: "Though many library users have needs that have changed in step with technological innovations, many have not, and we do a disservice to those patrons if we focus exclusively on keeping up with technological innovation."

When Library 2.0 was first being discussed in blogs, at conferences, and in libraries, there was some debate over the chosen name "Library 2.0"—a play on the term "Web 2.0." Some librarians also wondered why there had to be a name for it all, arguing that there was nothing new about wanting to better serve library users. We could debate "Library 2.0" and possibly come up with any number of alternate names for this library service model. We also could talk ourselves in circles about how libraries have *always* had to change to keep up with users and that driving force of Library 2.0 is nothing new. But if libraries are already Library 2.0, then why are people not only still talking about it, but changing their services to become Library 2.0?

Here's why: Library users are changing rapidly; this is nothing new. Library services also have to change rapidly to keep up, but unfortunately, most libraries have not been able to do so. Library 2.0 is an attempt to focus our energies on two specific objectives—empowering the user and constant change—in order to keep up with the changing needs of our users. Additionally, libraries have never been able to consistently reach the Long Tail of users who are not using our services. The elements of Library 2.0 help us meet this goal. So, while the goal of Library 2.0 to reach and better serve library users is not new, the combined elements of the Library 2.0 model can help us reach it.

TRADITIONAL VS. NEWER SERVICES

Every service we offer must work toward fulfilling the library's mission. Any service, new or old, may be able to accomplish this. Innumerable libraries perform traditional library services that are being well received by library users, just as there are libraries crafting new, technology-dependent services that are also successful at meeting user needs. Old or new, the ultimate success of any service is determined by the library user.

And, that's the key. For Library 2.0 to meet its goal of better library service, no service can continue forever without being reviewed to ensure it is still successfully serving library users. No service can be truly successful without some level of feedback or design assistance from the community the library serves. Reaching out to the community is critical to any successful service, whether through a traditional book club or an online catalog that accepts comments and ratings.

Your users will ultimately determine the mix of traditional vs. newer services that you offer. You will probably find that each age group and each demographic wants a bit of a balance between the old and the new. On a recent visit to ImaginOn, the Public Library of Charlotte & Mecklenburg County's exciting new 100,000-square-foot facility dedicated to serving the youth of Charlotte, I was amazed to see amid the high-tech learning tools a number of teens playing old-fashioned board games, reading books, and playing cards. Kids certainly enjoy interactive computer games and multimedia presentation centers. But they also like drawing and painting and writing stories of their own. Likewise, teens love X-Box gaming and RuneScape tournaments, but they like more traditional library offerings as well.

Library users will almost always want a mix of services. Though we may strive to become more than "brand book," the fact is we will *always* embrace brand book; we just don't want it to be our *only* brand. But just as we argue that we need to reach out with the newest technology at our disposal, so too should we continue to reach out with those services that continue to serve our users so well.

Technology's advances over the past two decades, and especially over the past few years, have caused many librarians to fear that their services—library services—would no longer be needed. The introduction of computers into libraries, the very quick development of the Internet, and the almost overnight expectation that libraries would provide Internet access—all of this was too much for some. Many librarians were pushed out of their traditional comfort zone, and some have not felt well since.

But the OCLC survey—and indeed our own local users—reminds us day after day that there remains a place for traditional library services. Though these may be augmented and supplemented with electronic resources, the work of the traditional librarian will always be needed. We need to be careful, though, to keep in mind the expanding role of the library. A well-structured organization that incorporates change into its operational structure will have an improved chance of weathering whatever changes come next. We will always be needed for reference work, literacy education, and the myriad other traditional services we offer. What one library system does will not always work for another. Again, the collaboration of staff and community will help you determine what works and what does not. We just need to be willing to adopt new services and to change those already being offered, in order to bring back that comfort zone. If we are ready for change, then change will not prevent us from serving our mission.

ENDNOTES

1. Rick Levine, Christopher Locke, Doc Searls, and David Weinberger, *The Cluetrain Manifesto: The End of Business as Usual* (Cambridge, MA: Perseus Books, 2000): xi.

2

The Essential Ingredients

"I think that librarians need to pay attention to trends in the larger society and changing patron expectations. We need to throw out the phrase 'But we've always done it this way!' and think instead about what we COULD do, how we can reallocate resources and staff time and decision-making power to serve our changing populations."
—Rachel Singer Gordon

Chances are you're reading this book because you seek advice on how to improve your library's service and better reach your customers. As discussed in Chapter 1, there is a growing need for libraries to respond to customer demands more rapidly and to increase the response time in service creation. How do we accomplish this? Library 2.0.

Library 2.0 is a model for library service that enables libraries to respond to constantly changing customer demands. By utilizing the underlying principles of Library 2.0, we can bring ourselves closer to meeting the needs of our customers while expanding service to reach more users. By better understanding the components of Library 2.0, you will be able to begin implementing these changes into your organization. In order to give you a "big picture" conception of Library 2.0, in this chapter we will provide an introduction to its main components;

in the following chapters, we will discuss each component in more detail.

Library 2.0 is a model of library service that includes constant and purposeful change and user participation in the creation and maintenance of services, while maintaining a primary goal of extending the library's reach to potential library users. Implementing a system of change and participation will enable you to expand your user base and reach those customers you previously have not been able to reach. This model also calls for libraries to keep up with rapidly changing technology, social trends, and customer expectations, something libraries must do to remain relevant. Although these concepts of change and user involvement are not necessarily new, using them together in a Library 2.0 environment will help you keep your library relevant in the wake of the rapidly changing needs of your customers.

CONSTANT AND PURPOSEFUL CHANGE

Change is a primary component of Library 2.0. Let's be honest: If your organization is not open to change, your library has little hope for survival in the imminent future. Being wary of certain types of change is normal, but running from change does a disservice to both your staff and your customers. When we discuss constant and purposeful change, we do not mean change just for the sake of change. Constant and purposeful change is just that: constant *and* purposeful. While change can be disruptive, it does not have to be difficult—or painful! If implemented correctly, change will almost always be positive for your organization and users. One way to ensure that change is both constant and purposeful is to build the process of change into your organizational structure.

Change can be hard enough, so it is understandable that the thought of "constant change" can be terrifying for those who have had bad experiences with change in the past. An organization that employs a method for continual change in a way that is purposeful and clearly explained will have more success than an organization that randomly changes things on a continual basis without reason. To be clear, Library 2.0 calls for the former, not the latter, type of constant change. One particularly benign and fairly painless type of constant change utilized in a Library 2.0 organization is the continual process of reviewing and updating services. This type of change is not quite so scary to staff and customers as others can be. All you are doing is reviewing services to determine whether or not they are still relevant to library users, determining what could be done to improve them, and then making the necessary changes. As described in detail in Chapter 4, this type of constant change is carried out in an organized way that will create less stress and more success.

Constant change can be disruptive for staff and customers, but it does not have to be scary. It is important to implement a process for constant change that will be sensitive to the human fear of change while not sacrificing its positive aspects for your organization and its users. Again, libraries should not change simply for the sake of change. Not knowing why something has changed is the most common cause of anxiety in the wake of change. In order for change to really be effective and positive, the motivations behind each change and what it is expected to accomplish must be clear to all involved.

You may believe that your organization already has a successful process in place for implementing change. If this is the case, Library 2.0 will provide additional ways for you to verify or fine-tune this process to ensure the change you implement is always purposeful and that it covers the broad spectrum of library services and operations. For the rest of us, however, Library 2.0 can introduce us to a process of change that will help us reevaluate our services so that we can better meet the needs of our users.

The benefits of a Library 2.0 method of constant change can be seen when compared to the method of "Plan, Implement, and Forget" that many libraries currently use. Plan, Implement, and Forget occurs when a library decides to start a service, plans for it, rolls it out—and then promptly forgets all about it. When this happens, it does not take long for library customers to forget about the service as well. In contrast, a method of constant change that requires regular evaluation of all library services will better serve both your customers and your staff. The pitfalls of Plan, Implement, and Forget are further discussed in Chapter 4.

Libraries must continually evaluate services, procedures, staffing, and other library operations, and make changes whenever necessary, in the hopes of making the library better for both the organization and its customers. Nothing, except for the process of change, is constant, and everything is open to evaluation. Change must be acceptable for all levels within the organization; nothing is sacred. The model for change should be both vertical and horizontal, cutting across staffing, procedures, and services. Your organization should continually evaluate everything, looking for ways to update and improve. We discuss constant change and the process for implementing a system of change in your organization in Chapter 4; however, this is not a book on managing change. We simply hope to give you a good base for understanding the ways that change can improve your organization and also help you to better reach your users.

USER PARTICIPATION

User participation can enrich the programs and services your library offers. When we refer to user participation, what we really mean is customer involvement in the creation and evaluation of programs and services. This does not mean that library customers must have direct control over the creation or evaluation of everything at your library. What it does mean, though, is that library users should at least have an effect on the programs and services your library provides.

The level of customer participation will vary depending on the organization, the community served, and the service or program involved. Examples of user participation include customizable interfaces, tag creation, and writing reviews or providing ratings of materials within the online catalog or library Web site. A personally customizable interface would enable the user to design what library news, services, programs, or materials he or she will see on the library's Web site. My Yahoo! (my.yahoo.com) and Google News (news.google.com) are popular examples of customizable online interfaces. The tagging of items has gained popularity through such Web sites as Flickr (www.flickr.com) and Amazon (www.amazon.com). Tagging, or the submission of keywords to describe a particular item, gives users the ability to assign their own keywords beyond what librarians typically use: subject headings. This personalizes the catalog for library users. Some libraries are already allowing library users to write reviews or rate items in their catalog; other customers can use the feedback left by others as a form of readers' advisory—much as we have seen on Amazon for years. Ways your organization can promote user participation are explained in more detail in Chapter 5.

User participation can also include feedback through user and staff surveys. When seeking input on services and programs, it is important to gather feedback from both your customers and your staff. This will help you understand how the service is working for those teaching and sharing the service, as well as for those using it. In many ways, staff feedback is equally important as customer feedback. Library staff who provide direct customer service are the ones teaching the service and fielding complaints, suggestions, and comments. They are a valuable resource for finding out what your customers want and need. Both positive and negative customer and staff input will enable your organization to understand what works and what does not work when offering a service. It is imperative that your organization provide a way for your users and staff to give their feedback so that you can better understand the needs of your users. The importance of knowing your market and ways to achieve this is described further in Chapter 3.

REACHING YOUR CURRENT AND POTENTIAL USERS

Libraries have a strong base of regular users and a much weaker group of sporadic users. We also have within our communities a very large population of library nonusers. We know from numerous surveys, including the 2005 OCLC report *Perceptions of Libraries and Information Resources*, that we serve our regular users rather well. Those people who use our services on an ongoing basis are, for the most part, currently happy with what libraries have to offer. We are not perfect, but we do a decent job.

Library 2.0, though, is both about keeping our current customers satisfied and reaching out to serve the broader market. Through constant change, we can try to keep up with our customers' changing needs. With participatory, customer-driven sources, we give our users more control over the services we offer and the ways they are used. But what can we do to reach out to that large group of nonusers? As librarians, we wonder, "Why aren't we reaching those not using our services, and what do we have to do to reach them?"

If we limit ourselves to "brand book," as the OCLC survey illustrated, then we are forever limited by constraints of space and money. It is impossible for any library, no matter its size, to house every book that every person would ever want. But we are trying to increase our brand beyond that of the physical book, and this desire fits perfectly with our goal of reaching that huge group of nonusers—what has become known as the Long Tail.

The idea of the Long Tail is based on one primary reality that is true for any physical library building: Shelf space is limited. As a result, we can only keep what is most in demand by our users. By only keeping what is most desired, we are choosing not to house less popular titles that appeal to a broader spectrum of readers. The untapped masses desire more esoteric titles, but, when looked at in whole, the demand for these titles is greater than the demand for hit titles. To paraphrase Chris Anderson, author of *The Long Tail: Why the Future of Business Is Selling Less of More*, Amazon sells more non-hit books every week than Barnes & Noble sells books in total during the same week. Simply put, the quantity of people seeking less popular titles greatly outnumbers those seeking popular titles. If you just serve those seeking popular titles, you are failing to reach an entire segment of your user community. We will take a more detailed look at the Long Tail and libraries in Chapter 5.

There are ways that libraries can reach the Long Tail of users. Many new Web 2.0 technologies allow libraries to reach out to current users—and to find new ones as well. Netflix (www.netflix.com) uses the Long Tail theory to reach a market underserved by its local video rental stores. Far greater title choice and fast home delivery has equaled success for this company. Amazon uses this same model to sell millions of books that Borders and Barnes & Noble cannot stock in their physical stores, due to space limitations.

Now libraries are seeking to harness the Long Tail of their own users. Some libraries are beginning to offer downloadable media, giving library users access to a selection of titles that they do not have the room to physically house. Downloadable media provides increased access to audiobooks, films, and music for library customers. These new services are far from perfect—downloadable audiobooks are handicapped by restrictive digital rights management (DRM)—but they serve as a proactive attempt to reach out to new users and remain relevant to current ones.

In a way, libraries have attempted to reach the Long Tail for years through services such as interlibrary loan, which is often a primitive attempt by libraries to reach a broader audience. Costs and complexities, though, are painfully high, and the opportunity costs are abysmal. Some libraries are beginning to think outside of the interlibrary loan box and purchase used books via Amazon and other online retailers in order to fill title requests more quickly and cheaply. By carefully using seller descriptions and buying only from sellers with a high number of positive feedbacks, a library could often buy used books at a savings to fill its interlibrary loan requests. Librarians can then decide whether to add an item that was purchased in place of an interlibrary loan into the collection after it is returned, reducing the number of brand new titles that need to be purchased. This was not possible with the traditional interlibrary loan system.

Libraries can also reach users by expanding services offered in the physical building at a lower cost. One such example would be word processing and other office productivity software. Online Office-style applications, including word processing and presentation creation, allow libraries to direct users to free and low-cost online productivity tools that we previously would have had to purchase, license, and maintain.

You can proactively attempt to reach new users and improve your service offerings by testing or implementing these types of service changes. Judicious use of online Web 2.0 technologies allows libraries to reach out to new users. The use of technology to further your library's reach to potential and current users is further examined in Chapter 6.

The needs and wants of library users have been changing for decades. Libraries have tried hard to keep up, and, in some ways, have succeeded. However, we are now at a point where if we don't make significant changes in the way we create and maintain services, we will lose our relevance for the majority of library users. This is particularly true for public libraries. Implementing a model for constant change and user participation, both of which are multifaceted components of Library 2.0, will enable libraries to expand their user base and reach those users they haven't been able to reach. Putting the concepts of constant change and user participation together bring us to Library 2.0—the next generation library.

3

Finding the Road to Library 2.0

"We need to examine and if necessary redefine ourselves relative to our individual communities. There is no one solution that would fit all libraries."
—Martina Kominiarek

Each library will map out its own unique route to Library 2.0. How Library 2.0 will work within each organization will vary, based on that library's community and organizational structure. Because Library 2.0 can look different for each organization, it is important to know where your library is now and how your users are being served, as well as what your customers want and need, before trying to become Library 2.0. To do this, you will need to take a hard look at your organization. In this chapter, we will discuss the first step necessary to working toward Library 2.0: understanding your organization and your community. You must figure out where you are now, before you can know what you need to do, to get to where you want to go. We discuss the importance of understanding the needs and wants of both your current users and those who are not using your library before making changes toward Library 2.0.

WHERE WE ARE NOW

Libraries play a crucial role in our communities. A library is created and maintained to provide service to its users, whether it is a school media center, a college library, a public library, or a special library. Librarians and library staff have a vested interest in serving their customers; they provide the very reason for our existence. Over the years, libraries have developed and maintained services that many now consider to be essential elements. It is because we care so much that we fiercely protect the tried-and-true services we view as fundamental. Unfortunately for both our customers and ourselves, however, if we do not routinely verify that the services we offer are still the services our users want, we can lose our relevancy and usefulness to those we serve.

The desire to keep up with our customers' changing needs led librarians to the Library 2.0 discussion. Libraries have spent the past two decades adding new technology-based services, such as online catalogs, computers with Internet access, and self-checkout machines. Today, you can find these three services in many, if not most, medium-size and larger public libraries in the U.S.

Libraries add these technologies because they rightly believe that these services enable us to better meet our customers' needs. Through the advent of online catalogs, library users can quickly search for items that their library owns. With just a few keystrokes, I can determine whether my library has the latest John Grisham, if it is available for checkout right now, and where in the building it is located. And I do not have to be in the library to use this service; I can find all this information from the comfort of my own living room. Not everyone, though, has Internet access at home or their place of employment; those seeking free access to the Internet can often find this service at their local public library. Indeed, while Internet-enabled computers in libraries were once a new, luxury service, this service has today become almost as expected as the service of lending books. By adding computers with Internet access, libraries were able to keep up as society became more heavily Internet-dependent. By the same token, self-checkout machines have rapidly become part of the regular shopping experiences of millions of Americans. Many libraries have followed suit by purchasing self-checkout machines, hoping to decrease the amount of time customers have to spend standing in line and to increase customer privacy, all while freeing staff to more efficiently serve customers. Although not all self-checkout machines have been quite as easy to use as we would hope, as with many new technologies, second and third generation incarnations are often better than the original. Libraries implemented online catalogs, Internet access, and self-checkouts with the hopes of better serving our users, and, ultimately, these technologies helped us do so.

What the previous examples demonstrate is that libraries tend to be willing to adapt to the changing needs of their users. Certainly, we want to provide the services library users desire, even if we can't always do so. Librarians say:

- "We try our best to listen to patron suggestions and take their needs into consideration so that we can provide the best service to them we can."

- "We may not always be the first to offer a new service, but we do try to weigh the benefits and costs of any new service and change accordingly."

- "We try to [offer what our users want], and if we learn of a service that people want, we work to accomplish it."

- "We try aggressively to anticipate patron wants and needs, and provide for them before a patron can vocalize an interest."

- "My library does respond to user concerns and requests and previous surveys indicate the library is doing its job reasonably well, but there is always room for improvement."

Unfortunately, we can't always offer the services that our users want, often due to budgetary or bureaucratic restrictions. In today's world of limited funds and reduced staffing, how can libraries reach out to users and offer the services that they want? Librarians report:

- "There are many services we cannot afford or do not have the staff or expertise to implement."

- "Like most, our budget is not big enough to offer all the services we should for our students."

- "Often we are not nimble enough to 'strike while the iron is hot.' We miss many opportunities to provide service due to bureaucracy."

- The services that our users want cannot be supported by the funds we're able to raise. We do what we can with what we have."

- "We know of services that we want to offer, and that our patrons have said that they want, but we're on hold with those services right now due to budget problems."

So, what do you do when you want to offer a service that your users desire, yet you run into monetary, staffing, or bureaucratic issues? There could be many answers here, and no one right way to proceed. However, one suggestion we can offer for those with limited staffing and finances is to reevaluate those services you do currently provide. Do you offer any services that are expensive or time-consuming for staff but that are not well used by your customers? As one library staff member told us: "We have begun asking what we can stop doing, in order to do what we envision we need to do to be relevant in the future."

Even activities that are considered an integral part of traditional library service, such as interlibrary loan, can be a budget and staff hog—yet often satisfy very few customers. If this is the case in your library, think about what other more affordable ways you could use to meet the needs of those customers who use interlibrary loan. By reevaluating your current services, including those "sacred cows," you may be able to find some ways to cut costs so that you can provide other services that are more desired.

Dealing with bureaucratic issues can often be more difficult than dealing with budgetary constraints. In this situation, often the only thing you can do is document users' needs as best you can and present this information to whoever is preventing a service from being implemented. Hopefully, by proving that the need is real, you will be able to convince those in charge to let it happen. Fighting for our users is one thing that librarians do best.

KNOWING YOUR USERS

Who are your current users? Who in your community is not using your library? Who are the political leaders? Who controls funding or influences library policy? Before working toward Library 2.0, you will need to figure out the answers to these questions. In this section, we discuss the importance of building the library's mission around its community and a few ways that libraries can learn about their users' needs. Libraries should be aware of their users and their market before implementing a plan for significant changes.

Most libraries do have some method in place for getting customer feedback or figuring out what their customers tend to want. These range from user surveys, to researching trends in service use, to looking outward at what other organizations are doing to reach customers. There are many ways to learn about your users' needs, so if your library isn't yet doing something to solicit user feedback, you must start now. You will also need to think about getting feedback from those who are not using your library. Public libraries may find a sense of ownership from their community, even among those who are not regular library users; this makes it less difficult to get input from nonusers, if you simply ask for it. For the rest of us, seeking nonuser input may not be so easy. Be it a public, school, academic, or special library, each organization is likely to have its own special challenges in getting input from those who do not often use library services.

We had one school librarian tell us that her library does not have any nonusers, as all of the children in her school are required to visit the library as part of their regular schedules. Although this technically does make library users of all the students, it would be amazing if each of these students also finds what he or she wants from the library. This school library may well find a service it could offer that would increase the satisfaction of those students who visit the library only because they are required to do so. If you do happen to work for an organization that is fortunate enough to have no new users to reach, then you will have to fight only the half of the battle that involves keeping current users satisfied. Most of us, though, will have to figure out both what will keep our current users satisfied and what services we can offer that will turn those who are not currently using the library into customers.

Much of Library 2.0 involves building change around the needs of your community of users. What works for one library may not work for another. Because of this, we need to be careful when crafting services. It can be extremely beneficial to look at what other libraries are doing when thinking about ways to better serve our own library users, but we should always consider whether a service that works elsewhere will work in our own library. We need to look at many factors, including budgetary, staffing, and community needs. A library with limited financial resources may not want to purchase an expensive catalog interface overlay such as AquaBrowser Library (www.medialab.nl), even if this has been a well-liked service at the neighboring county library. Sure, library customers may appreciate the visual features and ease of use of an AquaBrowser-type catalog interface, but if funding is already stretched to the point that other more immediately needed services are not being offered, it probably would be a less-than-wise investment. Similarly, if you are in an extremely computer literate community, you will probably want to avoid spending an extensive amount of staff time and resources to offer computer courses that are likely to attract only a few participants.

We know that it is important for libraries to consider the needs of library users before, and as an impetus for, making any significant changes. We also need to learn more about our market and other places people may go for similar services. How do we gain an understanding of what exactly our users need, who else can meet these needs, and which needs we are actually capable of filling? We will discuss several ways to keep abreast of the changing needs of library users and our competition, and it is possible that your library is already using some, if not all, of these methods. We need to use the information that gives us a big picture look at what our users need and enables us to figure out which services will meet the various demographics of our community to create a plan that will bring our libraries closer to Library 2.0 and to better serve more of our users.

The Library's Mission Statement

Before discussing ways to gather data about library customers, we want to talk about the importance of library mission statements. When thinking about changing to meet the needs of library users, libraries must consider their stated missions. This is not a way to determine your customers' needs, but rather a reaction to their needs. How is your organization going to serve its customers? A library without a clear mission is like a boat without a captain. Your mission will drive your organization, serving as a guide when selecting services for your users and letting you set a clear course for Library 2.0.

When researching this book, we were amazed at the number of libraries that had fabulous Web sites but failed to include a clearly written statement of the purpose or goal of the library. This statement, often referred to as a mission, vision, or core value statement, should be prominently displayed and available on your library's Web site. Libraries create these statements as a way to publicly declare their core value and purpose within the community they serve. As this is a statement to your users, you should be sure that your users have easy access to it. Post it, not only on your Web site, but also in your physical building(s), where it will easily be seen by customers. If your library does not have a mission statement, or if it is outdated or no longer accurately reflects your community, then creating one should be your first priority. Every library, from school to academic to special to public, should have a stated mission. If your library is in an area with rapidly changing demographics, the mission statement should be revisited every few years to ensure that it is still a perfect fit for both your organization and the community you serve.

Examples of Mission Statements

The purpose of the mission statement is to broadly state the library's main goals or purpose for library users. The mission statement doesn't have to be very specific or include details, though some libraries elect to do so. It may be only a single sentence, or may be several paragraphs.

Examples of well-written mission statements include:

"The Ellsworth Public Library upholds the principles of intellectual freedom and the public's right to know by providing access to information, reflecting all points of view, for people of all ages. In addition to books and other materials of contemporary interest and permanent value, the Library provides and encourages the use of its facility, collection, and services to meet a wide variety of community needs." —Ellsworth (ME) Public Library (www.ellsworth.lib.me.us)

"The Mission of the Dallas Public Library is to link resources and customers to enhance lives. The Library is committed to inform, entertain, enrich, and to foster the self-learning process by facilitating access to its collections, services, and facilities to all members of the community. All service efforts will focus on customer expectations and needs. The Library will make available a broad spectrum of ideas reflecting diverse points of view and will provide collections that reflect the need and diversity of the community it serves. The Library will honor its public trust by assuring maximum use of public resources. Furthermore, the Library will stimulate the awareness and use of libraries to promote individual enlightenment, community enrichment, and economic vitality throughout the city." —Dallas (TX) Public Library (www.dallaslibrary.org)

"The Madeleine Clark Wallace Library serves the Wheaton community by collecting, preserving and building connections between the record of human knowledge and achievement. By creating a setting conducive to learning, discovery, and cultural excitement, we help community members meet academic and personal goals that extend knowledge and promote achievement in the individual and in the community." —Madeleine Clark Wallace Library, Wheaton College, Norton, MA (www.wheatonma.edu/library)

"North Harris College Library: The mission of the NHC Library is to promote life-long learning through exemplary service and instruction, library collections and resources, updated information technology, and physical facilities and equipment that support learning and meet the needs of the college and our diverse community of users." —North Harris College Library, Houston, TX (nhclibrary.nhmccd.edu)

"It is the mission of the Bloomfield Public Library to provide and promote open and equal access to the resources and services of the library in order to meet the informational, educational, and cultural needs of the community. The library seeks to encourage reading and the use of current technology for life-long learning and the enhancement of the individual's quality of life." —Bloomfield (NJ) Public Library (www.bplnj.org)

"We enable the people of our community to pursue lifelong learning through our responsive collections, electronic resources and innovative services. Our inviting public libraries are the cornerstones of our diverse communities where children and adults can experience personal enrichment and connect with one another. The District is guided by the principles of Public Librarianship and First Amendment Rights. The District protects library materials from censorship. We seek innovative ways to: Respond and reach out to serve the current and evolving information needs of our diverse community. Create a sense of community by providing a welcoming, inviting, secure environment for our public and staff. Provide excellent customer service that is both timely and confidential. Develop a well-trained, knowledgeable, courteous and professional staff. Communicate with our public and staff to ensure vital, relevant and effective library services. Manage our resources effectively and be accountable to our funding sources. We celebrate our accomplishments, learn from our mistakes and take pride in serving our community." —Las Vegas-Clark County (NV) Library District (www.lvccld.org)

"The Georgia Tech Library and Information Center is a creative partner and essential force in the learning

community and in the Institute's instructional, learning and research programs. The Library plans, develops and implements programs to provide expert staff, information, learning resources and information competencies to students, faculty, and staff and selected services to off campus clients. Using appropriate technology, the Library delivers resources to satisfy information needs, promote lifelong learning and create productive connections for the scholarly community."
—Georgia Tech Library and Information Center, Atlanta, GA (www.library.gatech.edu)

Community Analysis

Knowing your community's demographics and needs will assist you when deciding what direction your services will take and how you can best work toward Library 2.0. Much as you regularly review your mission statement, you must also often update your knowledge or understanding of your community, as your demographics may change. Other books cover this topic well, so we will not go into too much detail about creating a needs assessment or community analysis. The concept itself is simple yet important: Know your community and how well you are serving it. It's important to know about both those who are using your services and those who are not. Many library-planning programs often forget to include this nonuser polling component, and this is a mistake. What are the demographics of your community of users? Their educational backgrounds? Economic situations? Language barriers? There are numerous elements to the demographics of your community. A community analysis will give you a good idea of what those elements are, which you can then use to develop, evaluate, and update your services. As part of the community analysis, the library should take a good look at itself and whether the collection and services it currently offers are able to meet the needs of the community.

We recommend that a library do a thorough community analysis for each branch or library location at least every three to four years. With the rapid pace of change in our society today, going much longer than that between each analysis can cause you to miss significant demographic shifts in your area. You can use data from your county, city, state, or institution (if you are with a private or academic organization) to gain a better understanding of the demographic that you serve.

Drive-arounds, where staff actually drive around the area and note what they observe, can provide additional information about your community. For a college library, staff can walk around campus and see what the students are doing and where they are doing it. For a public library, staff can drive or walk around the area they serve. When touring your community, take notes on things like new housing developments, signs of overcrowded schools (such as trailers), shopping centers, daycare centers, retirement communities, or foreign-language signage; any of these can give you clues about the lives of the people who live and work in your community. For example, if you see a high number of daycare centers, this could mean that your organization is in an area with many families where both parents work. These parents may have a limited amount of time available to bring their children to the library. In this case, you could bring the library to their children through outreach to the daycare centers. Offer to come by with books and provide storytimes, and encourage daycare providers to bring children in for tours and programming. The valuable information gleaned from a community analysis speaks for itself. Hopefully, your library is already doing a regular assessment of the community and its needs. If not, the time to start is now.

User, Nonuser, and Staff Surveys

Gather feedback and input from those who use your library, those who do not, and those who offer your services—your staff. We agree with Tabatha Reed of the Trails Regional Library in Lexington,

Missouri, who told us: "Libraries should welcome comments and suggestions and periodically offer informal anonymous surveys and evaluations to the patrons. Keeping up with new trends and technology is extremely important to keep people coming to your library." You can gain valuable information by polling and surveying your customers. Just remember that formal information-gathering surveys that require several focused minutes of time can be tedious for both customers and staff (although these surveys can yield a lot of information if they are well designed and planned and not simply regurgitated year after year). Informal surveys can be extremely beneficial as well, and the fewer the questions, the more likely you are to get a good rate of response.

Conducting surveys on a regular basis can be beneficial for seeing trends. These surveys also provide information on your customers' needs and how well you currently meet them. Having a way for customers to provide feedback whenever they choose is equally as important and often quite informative. This indirectly solicited feedback, usually through such means as a customer comment card, online form or blog, conversation with staff, or letter to the library, provides a way for customers to give ongoing input. Your organization should encourage this feedback and provide an open, welcoming, and inviting environment in which people can submit it. If you can get past the fact that most comments will be negative—people seem rarely to want to comment when they are satisfied—you can gather interesting information on what your users want and what your library fails to provide for them.

Also develop ways to gather input from those not currently using your library. It sounds difficult, getting someone who never uses your library to talk to you about the library. Most nonusers you approach will say something like: "But I don't use the library, so I don't know anything about it, and I can't give you any feedback." This is a challenge, but persistence can pay off. Attempt a friendly counter to the previous statement, such as: "But what would bring you in? What could the library offer you that you could use? What do you pay for now that you would like us to offer you for free?" Another tactic is not to directly ask about the library at all. Ask nonusers questions like: "We know that you don't use the library, but what do you use? Do you go to a book-store or café? Do you like to download music?" This can apply to both current and potential users. Find out what they are doing that the library could offer them, for free and possibly better. These types of surveys could be conducted in person at public locations outside of the library, or through direct mailings or online surveys advertised on community message boards or in local newspapers.

Surveys are not always cheap, whether for current users or nonusers, but the payoff can be immense. You will gain valuable information about your community and the services they want. It is also important to note that direct feedback should happen on a continual basis, well after you've planned a way to work toward Library 2.0. This service model calls for the consistent use of current and potential customer input when crafting and evaluating library services.

The one thing we heard most from library staff was that administrators should consult staff when wanting to learn about their customers and their service needs. As one librarian told us: "Provide the staff with a voice. We're the ones who work with the library users on a daily basis, and we're the ones who have the best 'feel' for what their needs are." Indeed, frontline staff members are the ones who market the library and its services, and those who teach patrons how to use what the library has to offer. They are also the eyes and ears of your organization. Your staff members on the frontlines know what customers are asking for and what they are using. Survey the staff on a regular basis to find out what customers want. Build a bridge across any gaps between your library's administration and its staff; this two-way river of communication should always be open, not just when discussing customer needs and services. We further discuss staff involvement in the uncovering of what your users want and creating effective services in Chapters 4 and 8.

Library Use Trends

Your library's usage statistics can be a good indicator of the success of any service. Examples of statistics include circulation figures, door counts, reference transaction counts and question documentation, computer usage numbers, and program attendance figures. Many ILS systems today easily produce documentation, not only on overall circulation data but also on circulation figures by hour, collection, and checkout terminal. These details can provide answers to questions you may have about which collections or services are successful and why. If a service does not seem to have high usage, consider why this may be the case. If you have a low turnout for your classes on introductory computer skills, consider whether the classes are well advertised to those who need them most. Also ask yourself some hard questions: Is there really a need for this service in your community of users? Are the classes offered at a time when those who could benefit are able to attend? There are several factors in determining whether and why any service is successful; attempt to consider them all when completing an evaluation. Library usage statistics can assist you in a number of ways when trying to gauge the services your users want. These details can help you see the big picture of what your community wants and needs.

Usage extends to your online offerings as well. Powerful Web analytics applications like WebTrends (www.webtrends.com) can help you learn what your users are doing online. Want to know how many clicks it takes most people to get to your catalog or programming calendar? Interested in knowing what Web browsers are used to view your library's Web site? Web analytics software can help you. Another exciting tool from clickdensity (www.clickdensity.com) allows you to track a user's mouse movements—where they linger and where they click. If you're interested in learning just how usable your Web site is (or is not), this is the tool for you.

Looking Outward

Part of knowing your community is knowing what your users do when they are not in the library. Where else do they go for entertainment? Enrichment? Education? Find out where these places are, and see what you can learn from them. For example, if you ask any librarian,

"Where is another place that people go for information?" you will overwhelmingly hear the same response: the Internet. What we now need to do is find out what the Internet has that we can offer in our libraries (besides free access to the Internet itself), such as free online Web 2.0 tools. The Internet should not be considered an enemy or competitor. Instead, view it as a tool that you can use to reach your users. Suggestions for Internet and other technology-related services that can help you work toward Library 2.0 and reaching your users are found in Chapter 6.

Think also about places besides the Internet that people go when they are not at a library. Consider movie and community theaters, bookstores, or cafés. Would people in your community enjoy free classic movies screened at the library (popcorn provided, of course)? What about arranging free SAT, GRE, LSAT, MCAT, or other test-preparation services, something that often costs someone hundreds of dollars to get on their own? Are there things that your users do alone at home that they may enjoy doing with a group in the library, such as video or computer games? Several libraries have had success over the past few years offering gaming nights where patrons can come into the library to play electronic games together. You can come up with scores of ideas if you look outward at other businesses or industries. Don't think of your library as being in a "library" box. What are your users doing elsewhere that they could be doing through your library?

WORKING WITH YOUR COMPETITION

You must be a part of your community in order to have staying power. Your customers must feel a sense of positive ownership in your organization for it to survive. They must be willing to fight for you. It is important to reach out to everyone, including those you traditionally may think of as competitors for your customers' time. A significant part of Library 2.0 lies in making sure your library maintains a healthy relationship with your users as their needs change. Part of doing this involves building good relationships with the other businesses and resources in the community that your customers use.

As mentioned in the Looking Outward section of this chapter, it is important to consider outside sources of information and entertainment and their effects on our customers. Most of our customers lead busy lives with a lot going on when they are not using the library. For many customers, time is limited, and so is their attention span. After you have determined who your competitors are, form alliances with them. We often refer to other businesses such as bookstores or movie theaters as competition, and, in a way, they are our competitors for library users' attention. However, we can also take a positive approach. Befriend your competitors. Find out who runs the local bookstores and coffee shops. Set up joint events to draw in patrons. Planning an author event? Many libraries will host the event, while a local bookstore sells copies for authors to sign. Work with that local movie theater to show a classic movie during off-peak hours. Many theater operators will be happy to loan their unused space, give out coupons, and advertise their other movies to local residents. Creating a win-win relationship with local businesses benefits everyone.

Bookstores can also be a model for services that could work in your library. The so-called bookstore model does not always get positive reaction from librarians or library customers, which is understandable, considering it is a very untraditional way of providing library service. But even if you don't mimic the layout or shelving styles of book-stores, they can still provide hints on what services or programs could work for your library. Ask yourself why people often stay in book-stores longer. Is your library's seating as inviting? Is your lighting sufficient? Do you allow your users to drink coffee and other beverages, even if you yourself don't provide them?

GETTING TO LIBRARY 2.0

Knowing your community of current and potential users and what they want and need is the first step when thinking about how Library

2.0 can benefit your organization and its users. By successfully using the tools and methods discussed in this book, you will be well positioned to meet your community's expectations for excellent library service. Library 2.0 is inclusive, tolerant, and open-minded. Closed thinking need not apply. Are you reaching out to *all* members of your community?

In the end, Library 2.0 will look different for each library, based in part on users' diverse needs. Once you have a good assessment of your community of users, you can begin formulating a plan and brainstorming ideas for working toward services that can be called Library 2.0. Looking to other libraries and outside organizations can help you come up with ideas for new or improved service offerings that will better serve your current users and better reach potential users. While you can get great ideas from other libraries, it is important to remember that what works for one library may not work for yours. Also look outside of libraries to successful services being offered by other agencies and businesses. Be flexible and willing to adjust whenever necessary, and always consider the needs of your specific community of users when creating, evaluating, or updating services.

We discuss the elements of Library 2.0, including constant change and user participation, in greater detail in the following chapters. A good understanding of each of these will assist you when creating a plan for working toward Library 2.0. Buy-in is also critical to this process, and we discuss this in-depth in Chapter 7. The willingness to change and be open to new ideas will directly impact the success of your library.

4

A Framework for Change

*"If you offer all services, you can't focus on the most
needed. All services have to be evaluated by need, want,
and real cost."*

—Jo Ann Pinder

The ideas behind Library 2.0 are built upon the necessity for change:

- Reaching out to new users

- Building new services

- Responding rapidly to changing customer demands

Each of these requires organizations to develop the ability to quickly and regularly initiate change. Change, though, is perhaps one of the most difficult elements to design into an effective and flexible organizational structure. Organizations such as libraries tend to be strong and solid structures that, although designed to withstand the difficulties of modern government institutions, are not necessarily well situated to quickly and efficiently change to meet new market demands. Our staff and administrators easily fall into routines, depending upon tried-and-true services and methods of operation. What was once a new and unique service can very quickly become business as usual.

37

The purpose of this chapter is to assist you in creating an environment where customers and staff are involved in facilitating change and maintaining the ability to change at all levels. It is about taking the steps necessary to implement services, while at the same time establishing a regular process for reviewing and evaluating the worth and effectiveness of those services.

Although we discuss the need for change throughout this chapter and offer suggestions for bringing change to your organization, the topic itself is much broader than we can cover here. Appendix C contains a list of resources and suggested readings, many of which include more detailed information for dealing with and managing change.

Sporadic or Nonexistent Change

Many libraries build cycles of change into their organizational structure. We form teams to examine and respond to market demands, or because "it's time" to review the strategic plan or technology plan. These teams usually meet over the course of several months or years, and after careful deliberation, put forth a new vision or plan of action that is then sent out to the entire library or system for implementation.

This intermittent type of change, though, can be difficult. Staff members receive new directives, often including some rather fundamental changes in the way they perform their jobs. We then expect them to learn and become comfortable with a new method of operation, usually with little guidance, and any training may be rushed or incomplete. Fortunately, most workers are usually able to cope; though this can place them under an enormous strain, staff members will almost all pull through and meet the new expectations. Sporadic change, though, is unpredictable and tiring for all staff—which can have a significant impact on morale. Those who have been through one or more cycles of sporadic and disruptive change find it discomforting to know that, at some point over the next couple of years, they will be faced yet again with a radical shift in operations.

These sporadic shifts in response to new environmental inputs affect more than your staff; they affect your ability to respond to your customers and their ever-changing needs. As an organization, we become complacent with our current services; relying on sporadic change makes it terribly difficult, if not impossible, to quickly respond. Without a mechanism for review, services can go on and on without anyone thinking about their continued effectiveness. What is needed instead is institutionalized change, where everyone builds into their regular routine the expectation that (usually small, though sometimes large) changes will always be taking place.

Many organizations are currently using the method of "Plan, Implement, and Forget." If your library does use this process, you probably don't call it that, but it is easy to recognize when your library is stuck in this cycle. Here is an example: A library that uses Plan, Implement, and Forget will come up with an idea, such as starting a new instant messaging (IM) reference service. A team will come together to work out a plan for implementing this service. Once the plan is developed, the service is released (possibly on schedule, whether all the kinks are worked out or not). Its release sees either a soft (little advertising) or hard (lots of advertising) launch. Maybe a few months, or even a year, after the start of the service, someone reviews it to make sure it is still working properly and that the numbers support the need to continue offering it. And then … well, then we never again hear about evaluations of or updates to this service. The library still offers IM reference, but it is never reviewed and has basically been forgotten. This service has fallen victim to the process of Plan, Implement, and Forget.

Plan, Implement, and Forget does a disservice to both library users and libraries. The wants and needs of library customers are constantly changing. We must constantly change to keep them satisfied, so that they continue to consider the library to be relevant to their wants and needs. Libraries are also not served well by letting services become stale. Libraries need to keep their services relevant to library users, or risk extinction.

Libraries use Plan, Implement, and Forget for a lot of services and procedures, not just the library services and programs for our users. After their initial implementation, technologies, internal procedures, or staffing models are rarely reviewed. Library 2.0 provides a way for us to break this cycle and begin the regular review of all library services and operations. Once the system is in motion, it takes little staff time, given the amount of return on investment.

An Open Letter to All Library Directors

Dear Director,

As the person in charge, you have perhaps the best understanding of your organization's goals and you are empowered to coordinate change and innovation. Every suggestion here depends upon you for organization into a coherent, big-picture strategy.

1. *Move staff around.* While we would not want to encourage arbitrarily moving staff around, sometimes lateral transfers can be healthy for both the staff and the organization. This can be accomplished both in systems with several branches, where staff are given lateral transfers between branches, and in a main library, where a staff member is moved to a separate department. Although you would not want staffing to be so fluid as to prohibit stability within a branch or department, it is in a library's best interest to acknowledge the positive aspects of staffing relocations and transfers. Such change provides fresh perspectives and gives staff the opportunity to work with different management styles.

2. *Pull people together.* Have a big project? Temporarily relocate staff to improve communication and efficiency in order to get the project done. This can occur

on many levels. Administrative staff are usually already in the same building, in which case pulling everyone together should not be a problem. But when you identify who you want on your team (see the next few ideas), you may very well find that team members are split across locations. Bringing them together into one facility, even if only temporarily, allows for more face-to-face meetings, fewer misunderstandings and conflicts, and a better final product.

3. *Listen to your young people.* Young and new employees bring a wealth of ideas and opinions to their new positions. Harvest this enthusiasm by bringing several new staff into every project, every service creation meeting, and any other meeting that could use a shot of energy. Consider positioning them in areas that need improving, or bring them into headquarters and put them on a team.

4. *No one should inherit a position.* How often have we seen the following: You have a retiring department head who has been in her position for 10 years or more, and her second-in-command is automatically chosen to replace her. Maybe not the worst decision, but not necessarily one that will spark change and innovation. Instead, don't automatically move her executive officer into the position. Look outside the department for new blood, with new ideas, someone who is going to think outside the departmental box. You are bound to find a lot of talent out there in other departments, branches, or libraries.

5. *Change and innovation begin at the top.* Are you the boss, the director, the CEO? How often do you host brainstorming sessions? Do you sit in on departmental

meetings? If you make this a regular part of your routine, staff will grow accustomed to your presence, and, hopefully, be more open and honest in front of you. Try pulling in your younger staff and including them in your thought process. Give them an inside picture of your organization, and listen to what they have to say.

6. *Reward and recognize your change leaders.* Do you rate your management team on new ideas and implementing positive change? Are supervisors given real credit for innovating and improving library services? It is time to begin formally recognizing these talents and rewarding your employees for their originality and innovation. But make sure they know that leading a successful team that creates positive change is more important than simply tossing out new ideas every few weeks. Change is team-oriented, and those managers who can create innovative teams and nurture positive change are the most valuable.

7. *Create a team of eyes and ears.* Tap several staff members system- or library-wide and appoint them as your personal reconnaissance officers. Let them look for ideas for new services and ways to improve existing services. Give them the library car (or leave to explore) every three or four months, and have them visit other libraries in your region. Then, let them meet with you regularly every couple of months and listen to what they have to say. Keep your department heads out of this meeting so your recons feel free to talk about what they think needs to be changed. Be open-minded, because a lot of what they say will sound naïve and may call into question some fundamental principles under which you have always operated. Don't hold their enthusiasm against them, though;

this naiveté is exactly what you are looking for in order to break through traditional thinking.

8. *Nothing stimulates change like change.* When staff members observe new ideas being implemented, they see that innovation is recognized—and possibly rewarded. What methods do you have in place for fast-tracking ideas? Does everything have to go into the strategic plan, or do you have the flexibility to take an idea from one person or team and quickly pull together an implementation team? Set a goal of two or three fast-track ideas a year. Get them going, gather numbers regarding success or failure, and have a review team sit down and evaluate after six months. If it isn't working, kill it. Don't make a big deal out of failures. But, if it is working, then make sure that the entire system knows who came up with the idea—and reward that person or group in some manner.

9. *Frontline staff know your customers better than anyone else.* What are your customers saying? Face it, you don't really know. You may speak to one or two in the course of a day (often to those who are the most upset). You may have friends who visit your library and give you feedback. But you still really don't know your customers nearly as well as your frontline staff does. Frontline staff may deal with several dozen people each day, hearing every comment, suggestion, and complaint imaginable. Make it easy and safe for frontline staff to get their ideas up to you and your leadership team. And get those same frontline staff to pass along customer comments— not just those that customers take the time to write down, but the verbal comments and concerns that staff hear every day. Have a rotating team of one or two staff members from every branch location. Let them meet

quarterly and produce a simple report, so that ideas are mixed together and no one person feels like they cannot be honest in his or her communications for fear of retaliation. Read their reports and share the ideas with your leadership team. Much like your reconnaissance team members, try to be open-minded and see your staff's viewpoints and reasoning.

10. *Just do it.* If you attempt even just a few of these ideas, you will find yourself out of your office more—which is a good thing!

Sincerely,

Michael and Laura

INTEGRATING CHANGE INTO AN ORGANIZATIONAL STRUCTURE

You want to build change into your organizational structure. Constant, smooth change—evolutionary, not revolutionary—better allows an organization to move forward without the seismic fits and starts so commonly associated with the major upheavals of discontinuous change. But this type of change is not easy to institutionalize. In order for this smooth change to become a hallmark of your organization, you need to build it into every stage of your planning structure. This also makes your organization better prepared to deal with the occasional disruptive change that is bound to come along.

There are many ways to integrate change into an organization's structure, but one excellent way to do so is to create an environment where customers and staff are involved in facilitating change and maintaining the ability to change at all levels. This involves taking the steps necessary to implement services, while at the same time establishing a regular process for reviewing and evaluating the worth of those services. This method for institutionalized change follows a three-step cycle:

- Brainstorming for new and modified services

- Planning for services and success

- Evaluating those services on a regular basis

It is imperative that all levels of staff within the library have the opportunity to contribute and evaluate ideas and services for your organization. These three processes can be handled by vertical teams. Vertical teams are team structures that include staff from all levels of an organization—from frontline staff to the directorial level, and everyone in between. Vertical teams, like vertical communications, serve to flatten the organization, reinforce the sense of worth of staff from all levels of the library, and instill a sense of responsibility that everyone feels toward everyone else. You should also consider making all of your organization's teams and committees vertical, if they aren't already. It boosts morale when staff members know that their opinions count and that they can have an active role in the planning of library services.

Staff members have a lot to say about the changing needs of our users and about what services would be most successful, if we let them be heard. Several managers and administrators told us of the need to consult staff when making changes. Jennifer Jenness, technical services coordinator for the Williams Library at Northern State University, South Dakota, says: "Our staff are consulted and made a part of the decision on most major changes; minor changes are often left to the discretion of whoever will be most affected by them." One branch manager reports: "I depend on input and advice from my staff when making decisions: they've been here longer than I have, and they know more about the community. Their expertise is crucial."

While some librarians and library support staff reported that their administration welcomed staff input, many stated that they felt that their administrators or managers often do not care to hear their ideas or input. This occurs even though these staff members tend to have the most contact with customers and are thus in the best position to gauge what services the customers want:

- "There is a strong sense among staff here that a problem isn't a problem unless the director or a patron notices it. Staff concerns are often dismissed as idle complaints until a patron response form backs it up."

- "Although there are mechanisms for input and suggestions, things are mostly done/decided from the top-down and usually without true discussion."

- "The director claims to welcome suggestions but rarely follows up on staff suggestions; the vast majority of initiatives are proposed by him, the assistant director, and the systems librarian."

- "The staff are normally 'involved' (i.e., provide input) but we seemingly have little impact on what services, procedures, and other operations actually occur within the library."

One library administrator told us about the illusion of staff participation in change and administrative decisions: "One of the reasons I left my [previous] position was the illusion of participative management; administrators would ask for input, then proceed with what they'd intended to do all along. Decisions were constantly made that impacted the duties of frontline staff and angered patrons, yet staff were ignored when it came to making policy." This is a dangerous way for any organization to proceed. Once your staff realizes (and it won't take long!) that they are being misled to believe that their input is taken seriously, morale will drop, and you will receive no further feedback. This is obviously bad for both your staff and your customers, who in many ways rely upon staff to report their needs to those with the power to make final decisions.

With someone from every level involved, planning for any new service will be a much more open and inclusive project. Having front-line staff play a role in the planning and roll-out phases, as well as the training and post-roll-out evaluative phases, means that all staff will be discussing and thinking about the new service. This doesn't mean that everyone will be on board, but it does mean that no part of the process should seem "out of the blue" or be dangerously disruptive. Staff from every level will be stakeholders in the process and play a role in the project's success or failure. Sometimes incremental change is simply not feasible, and, the more open and inclusive your planning process can be, the greater the reward in the end.

Brainstorming for New and Modified Services

Ideas for change can be generated by both staff and customers. Find out what your customers want and need. Ask them for input about the services they would like to see. Make sure there is an easy way for library users to submit feedback. Also be sure that there is an easy way for staff to submit suggestions. Those who work regularly with library customers have valuable insight into what your users want.

Survey respondents were asked several questions about the atmosphere of change within their library. More than half of the participants felt that their library does not change enough. If library staff members feel this way, what do our customers think about our libraries' level of change? Are we keeping up with the changing needs of our users? Only 35 percent of respondents felt that their library consistently offers the services that library users want.

We did find it very encouraging that 35 percent of survey respondents report that staff members, not just administrators, are always involved in providing input or making decisions that affect services, procedures, and other operations within the library. However, the lengthier free-form responses to survey questions imply that many staff members do not realize that there are avenues for their input, nor do they feel welcome in providing feedback on services or promoting change within their organization.

In fact, several library staff members reported in the survey that they lack any avenue for submitting feedback or suggesting change within their organization. At the same time, however, many administrators reported that their staff has an easy way to submit suggestions. These avenues do often exist, but library staff is reluctant to use them for fear of rejection or of being ignored. Staff may also be unaware that they even have these opportunities for feedback, due to poor promotion or a lack of encouragement from administrators and managers.

Survey respondents offered ways that staff can initiate ideas for change within their own libraries. If you are an administrator or manager, encouraging feedback through similar avenues may increase the amount of staff input you receive:

- "Raise the issue in a library committee or staff meeting, raise the issue in a campus-wide committee meeting or forum, [or] raise the issue with a supervisor. It helps if the staff member bolsters his/her argument with proof that a change would help the library better achieve its mission and goals, and proof that other staff or patrons also want to see the change implemented."

- "It's as simple as bringing up an idea in committee meetings, department meetings, or with other staff members over lunch. Conversation sparks ideas, ideas are share[d] with more staff members, and change is planned carefully and implemented."

- "We have staff meetings once a month. If there is a procedure, policy, or service that a staff member would like to discuss, they bring it up during these meetings. Then, as a group, we make a decision. If a change is needed, that information is taken to the next board meeting."

Stimulating ideas for change from library staff can produce amazing results. Staff will be grateful and motivated by being a part of the process. Library customers will see an increase in useful and relevant services as the staff members they interact with pass on what customers are asking for and needing. When asked what stimulates change within their own library, survey respondents had interesting things to say:

- "Change comes from everywhere ... [T]he work environment is one in which everyone, from the administration to the student staff, is free to make suggestions and to be taken seriously. Our administration is very open and flexible to trying new ideas."

- "Oftentimes, change comes as a result of response to crisis or something that just isn't working. I guess you could call this user and staff feedback, but it's more on-the-fly than proactive."

- "Creative staff learn about new methods or technology from reading, networking, or attending conferences and lobby for change. Sometimes it is the administrators who instigate the change either by funding projects or cutting the budget."

- "At my branch, change can happen very quickly. We're a very small library with only two full-time employees, including myself. If we have an idea, or a patron has an idea, and it seems feasible and good, we often put it into practice that day. Some kinds of decisions and changes take longer, since they involve system-wide policy."

Don't wait for your staff to come to you with ideas; solicit them. Make sure there is an easy way for staff to submit feedback or suggestions. An administrator or director may not see herself as intimidating, but must still be sure to provide an open, welcoming way for staff to provide input. Several survey respondents felt that their opinions would be met with apathy or disinterest, particularly if the staff person making the suggestion was not a degreed librarian. This is unfortunate, as the perspectives of all staff, including those without a library science degree, are extremely valuable when creating and evaluating services and procedures.

Planning for Services and Success

Much as we have always done, we should continue to properly investigate and plan the services we will provide. Once you have a good group of ideas, you can evaluate each to determine its feasibility for your organization. It is important to continue to respond to the needs of your specific community. Just because an idea sounds good doesn't mean it will work for your particular library. That being said, it is still important to take all suggestions seriously. What may initially sound like a good idea, yet seems impossible to pull off, might turn out to be quite feasible after some investigation.

Although new technologies can help you reach users and improve services, be wary of making big purchases without first thoroughly investigating the technology. Don't fall prey to what Michael Stephens refers to as technolust—an irrational need to have new technology, whether or not your library really needs it. There is almost nothing worse than spending big money on a new technology, only to see it sit gathering dust in the storage closet six months later.

After your library has decided to implement (or significantly change) a service or procedure, the planning process should begin. It is important for all who have a stake in the change to be involved in the planning process in some way. Anyone who will either be affected by the change, or relied upon for the implementation or maintenance of a service, should be given a participatory role in the planning process. This role can often be filled by one representative from an affected department. You will want to incorporate the perspectives of all involved, including frontline staff—often the ones who sell a service to library users.

Let's say a library decides to implement a new downloadable music service. Who should be involved in the planning process? The collection development department will probably need to have a seat at the table, because they will be charged with researching available vendors and negotiating a contract. Do you have the bandwidth to provide this service? Someone from the technology department who knows the answers to technical questions like these should be involved as well. We do want this to succeed with the public, right? So, a marketing representative will need to be included. What about the frontline staff who will be promoting the service and instructing customers on how to use it? Depending on your library's size and situation, there may be more or fewer representatives—but you get the idea.

Evaluating Services on a Regular Basis

Be sure that you not only plan the implementation of the service but also plan to review it. In fact, in order to avoid the dreaded Plan, Implement, and Forget, you will need to create a review plan for all of your services. Even the services that you have been using with success for decades should be evaluated on a regular basis, if only to confirm that they are still needed or that they are working in the same way as originally intended.

One of the benefits of reviewing older services is that you often realize there are angles or aspects that have never been considered. As time goes by, a service that becomes forgotten or taken for granted can lose its luster. Staff may stop promoting it, and customers may no longer realize it even exists. By evaluating the service, you may discover a way to revitalize it—or may determine that these resources could be better used elsewhere.

When we asked survey respondents if their library regularly evaluates services and procedures, we received an interesting array of responses:

- "We try to, but it does not actually get done regularly."

- "We reevaluate when we prepare for accreditation, and on an ad hoc basis, but the latter case is more reactive than proactive."

- "An information audit is conducted very irregularly."

- "We conduct evaluations of services, but there doesn't seem to be a regular schedule or any constant procedure for evaluation."

- "Some are always in the process of refinement. Others sit for years and no one pays much attention."

- "Certain services are evaluated better than others. It often depends on the administrator."

- "We are asking for input more. We have teams formed to handle certain procedures, policies, and services."

- "Various committees meet on a regular basis to discuss policies, procedures, and services."

- "We are working on evaluations and discussing how to do this. We are also working on procedures and policies that support the changes happening in libraries."

- "I'm not privy to any routine evaluation of services, policy, or procedure—if it happens."

For those libraries that are already regularly evaluating all services and procedures, the move toward Library 2.0 will be much easier. For the rest of us, it is time to create a written plan. There are many ways to go about this, and your organizational structure will help determine what will work best for you. It is imperative, however, that no matter what your schedule looks like, it must include staff and customer input—and all staff should be well aware that these evaluations take place.

Every organization has at least one sacred cow, something that absolutely, positively, cannot be touched. This service is never questioned and is always expected to exist, whether or not it is being utilized to its fullest potential or remains a good use of resources. Sacred cows do not necessarily need to be eliminated; however, nothing should be protected from review. Everything should have a fair chance for evaluation and possible improvement or discontinuation.

THE THREE BRANCHES OF CHANGE MODEL

There are many ways to bring constant, purposeful change to your organization. Here we will describe one method that can be used to integrate change into the structure of a library organization, using vertical teams and the three-step cycle for institutional change discussed previously. The Three Branches of Change model allows all staff—from frontline workers to the director—to understand and see that change is a natural, positive, and expected part of the organization's life. It also includes input about any given service from both staff and customers.

Top-to-bottom inclusion occurs through the use of three very distinct vertical teams, each of which is charged with a specific and measurable task.

1. Investigative Team

2. Planning Team

3. Review Team

In this model, every customer or staff idea for new or improved service offerings and procedures goes through the investigative team for initial consideration. If the investigative team decides that an idea should be evaluated, for possible implementation, a planning team is then created and charged with gathering more specific data to determine feasibility. If the idea is determined to be feasible, the planning team then creates both a plan for implementation and a plan for reviewing the service after implementation. After the service has been implemented, the review team uses the review plan criteria that were set forth by the planning team to evaluate the service at regular intervals. Figure 4.1 demonstrates the flow of ideas through each team. While each service that is created or changed has its own new planning team, the library would have one ongoing investigative team and one review team, with membership rotated regularly at odd intervals. Any changes, stopping, or starting of services that require approval from administration, the director, or the governing board would be sent through the proper channels with the documentation supporting the requested change.

The specifics of each team in this model are explained further in the next few sections.

The Investigative Team

The investigative team, or I-Team, is the detective that must see the big picture. If a staff member or customer has an idea for a new service, it comes to the I-Team. If an existing service needs reevaluating, the I-Team handles it. Almost all change in the organization flows through the I-Team, and for very good reason. The I-Team is a vertical team, made up of staff from all levels. It is a large team, including several staff members. The team is charged with brainstorming new ideas, investigating current services and procedures, and giving initial consideration

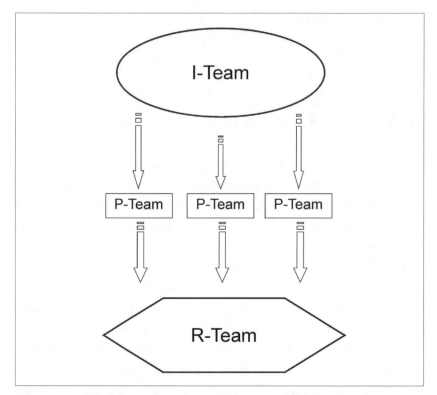

Figure 4.1   The Three Branches of Change example of vertical
            teams.

to service and procedure ideas from staff and customers. Membership should rotate regularly—each team member serving on a staggered one- or two-year rotation—so that many people will have the opportunity to serve. Not only will new faces bring new ideas, but staff involvement boosts morale.

All ideas for new services, whether from staff, departments, customers, or the I-Team itself, are funneled to the I-Team. The charge of this team is to identify what library users want, what needs to be improved, and what areas or groups need to be addressed. All of this requires input from numerous sources and levels, and this is where the vertical team concept pays dividends. When an idea is presented to the

I-Team, it is measured against many variables, including the library's mission, existing services, and service area demographics.

In order to meet its charge, the I-Team actually investigates each idea. The I-Team may find it useful to commission surveys, both internal and external, to measure demand or desire for a particular service. The I-Team may also want to visit other libraries or talk to organizations that have implemented services similar to the idea being investigated. Having frontline and administrative staff on the team will also allow for different viewpoints. The I-Team's ability to gather broad and accurate data is crucial; they use this data to determine whether the idea should move on to the next phase of the process.

If the I-Team decides that an idea would not be feasible at the current time, the process stops there, and a planning team for the idea will not be formed. If the I-Team decides that implementation should be investigated, a planning team designed specifically for that idea will be created. The I-Team creates a report comprised primarily of its data and reasoning and sends it to the idea's planning team, or P-Team. The P-Team uses this report as a starting point for its further investigation into the feasibility and planning of a service.

The Planning Team

A planning team, or P-Team, is created by the I-Team each time it requests investigation into implementing a specific service. After the P-Team meets its charge of further determining the feasibility of implementing the service idea and creating a review plan, the team will dissolve.

Like the other teams, the P-Team is vertical in nature but must also include interested parties, representatives of the departments that will play a role in the implementation and continued functioning of the service. What do we mean by interested parties? Let's go back to the idea of implementing a new downloadable music system. We'll assume that this idea has been put forth and that the I-Team has created a planning team to further investigate feasibility and create an implementation and review plan. While the P-Team should not be too large, any department that has a role to play in the success of this new service should be represented.

The planning team performs three tasks prior to implementation:

1. *Further determine the feasibility of implementing the service.* This will include a thorough review of the data set forth by the I-Team. The P-Team then seeks further data, such as implementation and maintenance costs, staff time involved, expected return on investment, and so forth. If it is determined that implementation should not go forward, the P-Team's work ends here. If the idea is deemed feasible, then it goes to the next phase.

2. *Create a detailed plan for implementation.* The implementation plan will be created with the assistance of all members of the team, which should represent all levels of your organization. This will include how to launch the service, whether training is needed, what kind of marketing should be done, timetables for progress, and anything else needed to implement this particular service.

3. *Design a review plan.* The P-Team will define the review criteria, such as statistics, user and staff feedback, surveys, or attendance. They will define what the review team, or R-Team, will use to determine the success of the service, with the understanding that other unplanned criteria might come up later and become useful in the review process. The P-Team will also create an evaluation schedule that will be used by the review team, including the frequency of review.

The Review Team

The review team, or R-Team, is also vertical in composition, and rotates members in the same way as the I-Team. As a standing team, the R-Team may find itself reviewing several services at any one time.

The R-Team is charged with carrying out the review plans set forth by the various planning teams in the organization and is responsible for all service reviews. Using the criteria and schedule for review that the planning team created, the R-Team analyzes and evaluates specific services in order to determine success. If, after reviewing a service, the R-Team finds that the criteria for success are being met, they do not need to revisit that service until its next scheduled review. If the R-Team finds a service is not meeting the success criteria laid out by the P-Team, it has to determine whether that service should be continued, modified, or stopped. The R-Team can also use the criteria that were laid out for success to modify the service so that it will better meet service goals. In determining a service's success, the R-Team will almost always rely solely on the P-Team's designated criteria for success. However, on some occasions evidence that was not included in the P-Team's original criteria may suggest success or failure.

Not all organizations will be able to follow the specific steps outlined for each process. Although this model may work well for medium- to large-size public and academic libraries, it obviously will work less well in a much smaller library with only a few employees. Some school or special libraries, or those with an administrative staff, board, or dean who are resistant to change will also likely have difficulty in enacting this particular model for change. Whatever type of library you are in, though, take two concepts from this process: the need for all staff ideas to be heard, and for all services, both old and new, to be regularly evaluated.

One way to become an organization that incorporates constant, purposeful change into its structure is to create a review process for your library's service offerings, which should be done in whatever way best suits your particular organization. Although the logistics of each team or method of service evaluation will vary based on your library's organizational structure, the spirit of this type of constant, purposeful change should remain the same: Customer feedback and staff input from all levels are imperative, as is the need to have a plan for regularly evaluating and updating all service offerings.

5

Participatory Service and the Long Tail

"Market, market, market. Get out there via blogs and RSS
and IM, and use some old-fashioned shoe leather and
elbow grease to put a face to the library, too."
—Karen G. Schneider

It will help us when we later define participatory service if we first look at the participatory Web. This relatively new phenomenon holds at its core the concept that users play an active role, not only in providing feedback, but also in the actual content creation of the Web itself. Far from simply being consumers, today's Web users actively add content, personalize Web spaces, and create structures that make finding information easier than ever before. Through the use of blogs, wikis, podcasts, tagging, and other ways of structuring data, it is now possible for users to have as much—if not more—control over the actual content of the Web than corporations with an official Web presence.

The participatory Web seeks to harness the power of its users in order to enhance content. We see this clearly on sites such as Amazon (www.amazon.com), where user reviews and tags completely alter the buying experience. No longer do consumers depend on only the seller's ad copy to make buying decisions; today's Web user has at his disposal the power of the community. We can read reviews by those who have already purchased the product or service we are contemplating. Poor product construction or lousy customer service experiences are now bloggable complaints and open for all to see. The strength of such communication cannot be overestimated, especially by companies trying to make sales.

An article at the *New York Times* Online that favorably reviews a new toy can easily cause the toy manufacturer's Web site to crash under the surge of traffic stemming from that article's readers. Likewise, a negative podcast that highlights a well-known Internet provider's abysmal customer service can quickly lead to blog posts and newspaper articles, which ultimately lead the Internet provider to issue a press release apologizing and promising to make fundamental changes to its customer service policies. Product recalls, customer service catastrophes, and celebrity gaffes are all fodder for the millions of sites trying to make their mark on the Web.

We used to say that television made news travel fast—and, at one time, it did. But television also condensed news into sound bites, small and often misleading phrases that conveyed no real information. The Internet, however, makes news delivery instantaneous, while keeping the content deeper, and perhaps more relevant. Readers have at their disposal entire articles instead of 30-second sound bites. A politician's factually misleading campaign statement is now immediately dissected and rereleased as news. Web sites such as FactCheck.org (www.fact check.org), run by the Annenberg Public Policy Center of the University of Pennsylvania, make it their duty to correct misleading political claims. Numerous other Web sites do the same for national and international news, consumer product claims, celebrity news, and the like. The participatory Web has limitless fact checkers, editors, and rewriters, making it almost impossible to lie to this new world of users.

We now live in a world often referred to as Business 2.0, where people and markets control the power. No longer do space and time play the limiting role they once did. Consumers can communicate and compare across such divides, making a company selling computers in Los Angeles a direct competitor to a similar store in Boston. Local markets give way to regional and international markets, where goods and services can be compared and purchased without regard to distance. Value and customer service, rather than location, are paramount to the buyer's decision-making process.

The idea of the participatory Web extends also to noncommercial Web sites that seek to be purveyors of information and knowledge. Wikipedia (www.wikipedia.org), for example, depends wholly upon its users participating and adding content to its enormous and growing online encyclopedia. Wikipedia allows almost anyone to add and edit content, trusting that the community of users will police the accuracy and authenticity of the information posted. Although Wikipedia has had to restrict editing on some pages to authenticated users only, this fails to take away from the online encyclopedia's ability to harness the knowledge of its users.

PARTICIPATORY SERVICE

Participatory service seeks to do for library services what the participatory Web has done for the Web itself. Users and their knowledge have the ability to reshape library services, but libraries must first change the way they craft their services and tools so that users have a clear and open avenue on which to communicate and participate.

For many years, libraries, like many businesses, were very unidirectional. Ideas flowed from the top down; services were created in high-level meetings, implemented by a few, and rolled out to a (hopefully excited) audience. But, more often than not, the services that libraries created served an existing user base. We created services for users when they were young kids, lost them as teens, got some of them back again as parents bringing their own kids in, tried to involve them in services such as reading groups, lost many yet again as they worked hard in midlife to save for retirement, and finally brought them in one last time as senior citizens, with targeted reading materials and programs for that age group. This is, of course, an oversimplification, but we have done better with some age groups and demographics than others. Teens, especially, seem to be our weak point.

In order for libraries to work toward a model of Library 2.0 participatory service, we must build mechanisms into our structures through which both users and nonusers can participate in the service creation process. There are many ways you can begin to build user participation into the structure of your organization. One time-honored method is through a simple customer comment card so often found in libraries. But today's libraries are also reaching out like never before, asking users and nonusers alike just what it is they want from their local library. Some, like the Waterboro Public Library in East Waterboro, Maine, are creating blogs that allow customers to comment on library happenings in the community (www.waterborolibrary.org/blog.htm). Others, such as the Darien (CT) Library, are creating blogs on which their directors post news and field questions and comments from the public (www.darienlibrary.org/directorsblog).

The comments and questions posed on these library blogs should then be discussed in meetings, and used both to improve existing services and to create new ones that fit within the library's mission. Incorporating customer comments into regular library administrator meetings is another way to listen to your public. Frontline staff who work with the public daily hear plenty of comments, many of them positive! These staff members should be encouraged by their managers and administrators to share their knowledge through regular meetings with top-level management, or encouraged to document the comments they hear, so that decision makers gain a better understanding of what the library's users are saying.

When your library plans new programs, whether you use the team method described in Chapter 4 or another method entirely, you need to build ways to include public comments and suggestions into the service-creation process. Simple surveying is one method, but another is to actively court local residents through outreach to civic and social organizations in the community. Make contact with people from your local Rotary, Chamber of Commerce, and other groups and ask them to sit in on some service exploration meetings. Get them to give feed-back about why they do or do not use the library. Not only will this give your library some valuable input, but it will also make community leaders more aware of just what it is the library actually does. The Library 2.0 idea of giving library users a participatory role in the serv-ices that the library offers—and the way those services are used—goes a long way toward making sure that the library is directing services to customers who will actually use them. By including nonusers in our service-creation process, we can be reasonably sure that we are craft-ing services they will desire.

Participatory service can extend to user customization of your cata-log and Web site. By allowing your users to tailor content and create personalized spaces, you relinquish some control over your site, but your customers will value the ability to make a corner of the library's Web site their own. Allowing customers to personalize their spaces encourages them to become regular users of your service.

It is imperative, though, that libraries consider customer privacy when creating participatory and customizable services. Public identifi-cation should not be obligatory for our users to participate in our serv-ices. Protecting our customers' right to privacy in technology-based services is just as important as protecting their rights when using tra-ditional or physical library services. Libraries can use some simple methods of helping to preserve privacy, such as allowing anonymous comments and content additions on library blogs, wikis, and catalogs. The preferred method of protecting user privacy is to utilize the opt-in method of participation and customization. This way, users have the option of sharing their data with others, without that decision being made for them. Users should not have to take action to protect their pri-vacy; they should only have to take action if they wish to share infor-mation that may be considered personal or private. Our Web pages, blogs, wikis, and other Web-based services should be fully readable and usable by all users without requiring them to opt in to any information-sharing agreement. The functionality of our Web pages, catalogs, and other electronic offerings must be maintained for users who do not wish to share their personal data.

THE LONG TAIL AND REACHING NEW USERS

The concept of the Long Tail, as explained by Chris Anderson, of *Wired* magazine and author of *The Long Tail: Why the Future of Business Is Selling Less of More* (Hyperion, 2006), is that the market for the non-hits—whether music, movies, or books—will always be greater than the market for the hits. Because brick-and-mortar businesses, though, have been unable to stock many of these items, we as consumers have had no real place to go to buy the very large number of nonhits.

What does Anderson mean by nonhits? Every year, a huge number of songs are released, only a small fraction of which get airtime on major radio networks and are stocked in local music stores. If only 20 percent of each year's music ends up in music shops, then the remaining 80 percent has basically been unavailable to the buying public. Niche catalogs, and, more recently, the advent of the Internet, have served to make this remaining 80 percent—the Long Tail, so to speak—more readily available. Conventional wisdom has it that Amazon sells more nonhits every day than hits, and since few of those nonhits are available from your local music retailer, this business is all going to the likes of Amazon.

Librarians like to pat themselves on the back and say, "Oh, we've always served the Long Tail." Sorry, but for the vast majority of libraries, this has simply never been the case. The Long Tail is more than simply a couple thousand niche titles tucked away in the stacks. The Long Tail includes 80 percent of the books printed *every year.* What percentage of these books does *your* library buy? According to Bowker, 172,000 new titles and editions were published in the U.S. in 2005; 206,000 new titles were published in the U.K. Still think you have a grip on that Long Tail? Not likely, unless of course your library rivals the Library of Congress.

Libraries, whether they want to believe it or not, are governed by many of the same rules as local retailers. We have a finite amount of space, shelving, money, and staff, and we are simply not able to house more than a small percentage of the titles printed every year. Very large academic libraries are a bit different, but they still cannot purchase the entire vast quantity of new books that are printed every year.

So, how do libraries attempt to serve this Long Tail? Libraries for years have attempted to serve it through interlibrary loan services (ILL), but this is an antiquated and expensive system of borrowing books from other libraries. ILL reached its peak prior to the advent of the Internet, when library users would find citations for books in bibliographies, union catalogs, and advertisements. Most libraries now no longer have to mail requests for items to lending libraries, instead being able to utilize online catalogs. But libraries are still required to mail items, and shipments and delivery times can range from a few days to several weeks during busy times of the year, when academic libraries are trying to serve their local population before addressing ILL requests from other systems. Even with electronic catalogs, the ILL process for most libraries is still painfully tedious and inefficient, often taking at least one full-time staff member, if not an entire department, to handle the service.

Some libraries are taking steps to change the ILL process, choosing instead to purchase used titles on demand from online retailers such as Amazon and eBay (www.ebay.com). If you choose to go this route, you may find success in purchasing used titles for pennies plus shipping. This can be significantly cheaper than the traditional ILL model. After an item is returned by the borrowing customer, your library then has the choice of either reselling that purchased item or processing and entering it into the collection for others to enjoy.

So far we have discussed the Long Tail of materials, but is there also a Long Tail of library services? Could we plot a graph showing that the desire for different services stretches out much like the desire for niche titles? We think we can. And, if we can, then how do we address that need?

Libraries are now considering ways to get the materials they already have to users who do not or cannot come into the library. Modeled on Netflix (www.netflix.com), and reminiscent of many lending programs for the homebound, materials can be packaged and shipped to users. There are several ways to provide this service, one of which is to offer to have new bestsellers, or any genre of materials, mailed to library customers for a fee. Examples include the hottest monthly suspense fiction releases being mailed to subscribing library users, with the subscription fee covering the postage, and, perhaps, a portion of staff time.

Another potential way to reach customers with physical services outside of the library is through Amazon's library processing service. Libraries could have processed books and other materials sent directly to a customer's home, and that person would bring an item to the library after using it. When a pre-processed item is returned, it would be entered into the library's circulating collection. Books would already have spine labels and Mylar covers, so no additional processing will be required. Even the MARC record would have been sent from Amazon, so the item can easily be placed in the catalog.

This Netflix model, as it's often referred to, does something few other services have been able to do: get materials into the hands of people who do not come into libraries. We've been able to push out our virtual services to these people, but rarely have we been able to get physical materials to them efficiently. Other libraries, such as Niagara University (NY) Library (www.niagara.edu/library/illdvds.html), go one step further than creating their own Netflix-like service, and are actually using Netflix to supplement their DVD collections (Figure 5.1). As part of this process, staff members first try to obtain the DVD from Netflix, turning to their traditional ILL system only if Netflix is unable to provide a copy. Interestingly, they promise three-business-day delivery with Netflix, but warn of up to a two-week delivery time for those DVDs that must be obtained through interlibrary loan.

What Makes a Service Library 2.0?

No single defining criterion makes a service fit under the banner of Library 2.0; there is no precise litmus test designed to identify Library

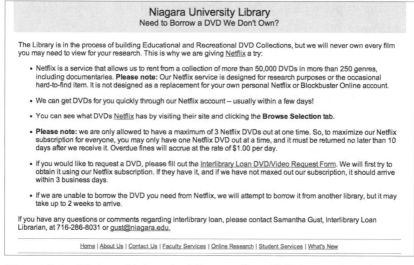

Niagara University Library
Need to Borrow a DVD We Don't Own?

The Library is in the process of building Educational and Recreational DVD Collections, but we will never own every film you may need to view for your research. This is why we are giving Netflix a try:

- Netflix is a service that allows us to rent from a collection of more than 50,000 DVDs in more than 250 genres, including documentaries. **Please note:** Our Netflix service is designed for research purposes or the occasional hard-to-find item. It is not designed as a replacement for your own personal Netflix or Blockbuster Online account.

- We can get DVDs for you quickly through our Netflix account -- usually within a few days!

- You can see what DVDs Netflix has by visiting their site and clicking the **Browse Selection** tab.

- **Please note:** we are only allowed to have a maximum of 3 Netflix DVDs out at one time. So, to maximize our Netflix subscription for everyone, you may only have one Netflix DVD out at a time, and it must be returned no later than 10 days after we receive it. Overdue fines will accrue at the rate of $1.00 per day.

- If you would like to request a DVD, please fill out the Interlibrary Loan DVD/Video Request Form. We will first try to obtain it using our Netflix subscription. If they have it, and if we have not maxed out our subscription, it should arrive within 3 business days.

- If we are unable to borrow the DVD you need from Netflix, we will attempt to borrow it from another library, but it may take up to 2 weeks to arrive.

If you have any questions or comments regarding interlibrary loan, please contact Samantha Gust, Interlibrary Loan Librarian, at 716-286-8031 or gust@niagara.edu.

Home | About Us | Contact Us | Faculty Services | Online Research | Student Services | What's New

Figure 5.1   Niagara University Library offers DVD borrowing via Netflix.

2.0 services. What makes a service Library 2.0 is the planning and structure built into it. That structure needs to include:

- *Constant change.* Is the service frequently evaluated to ensure that it is meeting its expected outcomes and that it is still relevant? When the service no longer meets its expectations, is it updated or replaced?

- *User participation.* Was customer input used in the creation of the service? Does the review process continue to include customer feedback? Are library nonusers asked to participate in the service creation and review process?

These elements are vital to maintaining a viable and well-received library service with Library 2.0. Reaching out to our users and building the ability to change into the planning and review process, and doing so with a mix of frontline and administrative staff, will allow your library to flexibly respond to changes as they arise. No service, no matter how great, can remain effective forever. All services need refreshing, updating, and sometimes even canceling. Having this structure in place plays a large part in being able to say your services are Library 2.0.

EXAMPLES OF LIBRARY 2.0 SERVICES

Ann Arbor District Library's Main Web Page

Under the leadership of library director Josie Parker and staff members Eli Neiburger and John Blyberg, the Ann Arbor District Library's (AADL) Web page (www.aadl.org) was selected by the American Library Association as the best Web site in the nation for libraries with budgets of $6,000,000.00+ (Figure 5.2).

Figure 5.2   Ann Arbor District Library home page.

The AADL Web site was created using Drupal and incorporates the ability for customers to comment right on the main page. In addition, the director maintains a blog, and the library catalog has a rather unique feature called Card Catalog Images that allows users to write marginalia on virtual card catalog cards (Figure 5.3). These images are then stored in the catalog user's profile.

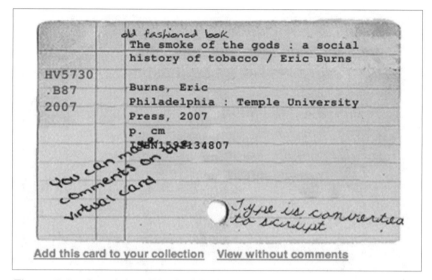

Figure 5.3   Ann Arbor District Library virtual card catalog. Customers may add marginalia and save these cards to their personal library page.

What makes this Web site Library 2.0 is not necessarily the technology itself, but what the technology gives the library user—namely, an easy means of communicating with the library and of adding and personalizing content on the AADL Web site. The technology is the tool that the administration employs to help them and their customers carry on a dialogue in the easiest manner possible. (Find more on the AADL site and external blogs in general in Chapter 6.)

Rock the Shelves from Gwinnett County Public Library

Held in the summer of 2005, Gwinnett County Public Library's (www.gwinnettpl.org) Rock the Shelves teen outreach event brought three local bands and more than 300 teens to the Lawrenceville, Georgia, library for an after-hours concert (Figure 5.4). This concert was put together in part by working with local teens and listening to what they wanted. With the support of local businesses, the library was able to provide food and drink for everyone in attendance. Each

Figure 5.4   Gwinnett County Public Library's Rock the Shelves
             band night.

participating band also received several hours of recording time in a
local recording studio.

SirsiDynix's vice president of innovation, Stephen Abram, wrote on
his blog, Stephen's Lighthouse (stephenslighthouse.sirsi.com): "You
gotta admire the creativity here and the crowds are obvious. Innovative
strategies for reconnecting with teens through events, MySpace
events/calendars and library blogs and Web sites needs to shared more
widely ... The strategies are about more than just gaming and DDR—
and those are cool too."

RSS Feeds from Tacoma Public Library

The Tacoma (WA) Public Library (www.tacomapubliclibrary.org)
recently began engaging its users by pushing content to them via RSS
feeds (Figure 5.5). By allowing its users to get content where and when
they want, instead of making them come to a building or Web site, the

Figure 5.5   Tacoma Public Library's home page offers RSS feeds.

Tacoma library is taking that giant step of putting itself where its users want it to be.

Darien Library Blogs

The Darien (CT) Library (www.darienlibrary.org) has 10 blogs available from its home page, including blogs for teens, for books, and a director's blog (Figure 5.6). (More directors should be blogging!) This library is using blogs to reach out to multiple interest groups, giving practically the entire community a way to interact with the library.

Figure 5.6   Darien Library's blog offerings.

6

Incorporating Technology

"We have to meet our users where they are with tools they can [use] and are comfortable using."

—Anonymous

Over the past two decades, the increasingly powerful technology available to us has changed the way libraries operate; we cannot ignore the enormous effect technology has had on both our customers and ourselves. Libraries are wise to embrace new technologies, though we must avoid the lure of technolust. As defined by Michael Stephens, technolust is "an irrational love for new technology combined with unrealistic expectations for the solutions it brings."[1] When incorporated wisely, however, technology can help us meet our Library 2.0 goals and allow for better, more efficient service to our customers.

The rapid pace with which new technologies are made available can be overwhelming, particularly for those who are less tech savvy or who must shop on a limited budget. Fortunately, many affordable or free services can help libraries increase their reach to both current and potential customers, as well as improve their service offerings. The new world of Web 2.0 technology is already having a significant impact on library service. Indeed, this new, changing world of technology will do nothing less than change the very way we do business.

73

A 2.0 WORLD

Since the late 1990s, businesses have experienced some rather fundamental changes in the ways in which they operate and interact with their customers. Customer, or user, participation has become essential. The role users play, both directly and indirectly, in corporate advertising, marketing, and customer service has expanded exponentially within just the past few years, and the Internet has been the primary catalyst for this change.

New business models have sprung from such companies as Flickr, Amazon, Netflix, eBay, and Apple's iTunes, and the term Web 2.0 has been used to describe some of these companies and their business models. As originally defined by Tim O'Reilly and Dale Dougherty, Web 2.0 says that the Web itself has redefined the way companies do business. Companies and their Web sites have become more open and interactive, allowing user input and customization and adopting a more open attitude toward information-sharing through the use of application programming interfaces (APIs). Content, or information, has become less centralized and isolated, as the old information silo analogy is replaced by the concept of Web sites as sources of content and knowledge that can be shared with other Web sites.

One way to share content through the use of APIs is by using mashups, where information from more than one source comes together within one Web application or Web site. This is well demonstrated through the mashups created with Google Maps (maps.google.com). Examples abound of real estate agents, demographers, franchise operators, and delivery companies, all overlaying their data or products on top of Google Maps so that their customers can better understand their geographic relationship to the company's product or service. In these examples, all three involved parties (Google Maps, the customer, and the company providing the data) benefit from the mashup. Google delivers ad content, the company pushing the data often increases sales, and the customer can better understand the product to make more informed decisions.

Also fundamental to the Web 2.0 idea is the importance of the conversation. The advent of such new tools as blogs, wikis, and other social software applications has allowed customers and corporations to talk and interact as never before. No longer must a telephone be dialed and answered, a stamp be purchased and a letter mailed, or a fax be sent and received in order for a conversation to take place. The costs associated with conversation have been virtually eliminated, and customers can now speak to a far wider audience than ever before to express their satisfaction or dissatisfaction with business.

The average information technology (IT) department is only now beginning to feel the impact of Web 2.0. Until recently, technology departments maintained a sort of absolute control over the services offered on their equipment. These departments had a set way of doing things, and were rather conservative and slow to change. IT has been accustomed to setting up computers and installing software, then walking away with some reasonable assuredness that the way they set up a computer would be the way it stayed. Even with the advent of the Internet and users' ability to download software, the average IT department could lock down the administrative settings on each computer so that very little could be installed without IT's approval. Web 2.0 technologies change this, giving users access to a wide variety of applications that are neither installed nor approved by IT.

Communicating with frontline staff and customers is critical to the successful operation of any library, but technology departments tend to be ill-suited to such give and take. Their rigid structures, firm expectations, and desire for stability over any interest in emerging technologies often make them difficult to change, especially when that change involves communicating with more people and gathering input from our users. The 2.0 technologies help bridge this divide by building the ability to offer feedback directly into the applications themselves. IT staff who are not adept at talking face-to-face with customers can now carry on that discussion through the use of blogs, wikis, instant messaging, and any number of other interactive and collaborative technologies.

Your library can use numerous low-cost and free Web 2.0 applications to expand its service offerings. Users, for example, now have access to powerful browser-based Microsoft Office-style applications. These applications can obviate the need for bloated and expensive software installations and the necessary updating, licensing, and, eventually, upgrading that come along with them. Web 2.0 tools such as Zoho (www.zoho.com) and Google Docs (docs.google.com) offer library users the ability to complete tasks that until only recently required library-installed software. Many libraries do not currently offer public-use computers with word processing and other Office-style software applications, or they limit offerings to only a few computers due to staff or budget constraints. Online applications can help fill this gap.

Products from companies such as 37 Signals (www.37signals. com) have begun to blur the lines between office, home, and Starbucks. You can now upload a Microsoft Word document, save it online, give access to any number of people, and then collaborate, often in real time, on that same document. This breaks down barriers of time and distance, allowing a type of collaboration and group work to which most people previously lacked access. Even Microsoft Office, despite its power, does not facilitate such easy collaboration. This also means that both library staff and library users can access these tools anywhere: on staff computers, on the library's public computers, and through the library's wireless connection. Everyone will soon begin to take for granted the ability to work wherever and whenever they please.

Although these Web 2.0 tools present an opportunity to serve more people with our existing infrastructure, they also present a new challenge. Most of these Web-based applications do not offer direct technical support. Customers who experience problems while using an application are often limited to submitting a feedback form or e-mail message to the company that created it. Response time will not necessarily be as fast as when seeking assistance from an on-site staff person. For this reason, libraries that choose to advertise and recommend Web 2.0 tools should be prepared to face the technical challenges that come with them. A good starting point is for your library to create and offer staff training on the use of popular Web 2.0 tools.

These free or low-cost and easy-to-use applications abound. In addition, higher-cost (but often more powerful) software is also incorporating Web 2.0 applications. An excellent example is Microsoft Office Sharepoint Server 2007, which, in its newest version, now incorporates RSS feeds, blogs, and wikis. Sharepoint is an extremely powerful, though expensive, application, but previous versions lacked the RSS feed, blog, and wiki components. While not many libraries can afford or need to purchase Sharepoint, the fact that Microsoft has placed these 2.0 tools into its product illustrates the essential position these applications now hold.

In addition to people being able to write and crunch numbers together, social networks have emerged as one of the most popular uses of today's Web 2.0 Internet. People from every demographic are enhancing existing relationships and crafting new, virtual neighborhoods through the use of such tools as IM, text messaging, online community portals, blogs, and voice over IP (VoIP)-driven applications like Skype (www.skype.com). Librarians are no exception to this trend and can be seen online in almost every major social network, using every tool available, and making their presence felt.

This ability to interact socially and across vast landscapes of space and time has had a direct impact on both internal and external business operations. Employees and customers can now communicate instantly and frequently with one another, setting up extensive new webs of interaction. This type of interaction can very easily eliminate boundaries between top-level management and frontline staff, leading to a flatter organizational structure—an important element of Library 2.0.

HOW LIBRARY 2.0 USES WEB 2.0

Library 2.0 is about doing more with the same or fewer resources. It's about efficiency without sacrificing quality. It's about reaching out to new users without losing those we already have. Many current and forthcoming Web 2.0 applications allow libraries to work toward the Library 2.0 model. With Web 2.0 technologies, we have at our disposal a vast array of tools that invite user participation. If used properly, these Web 2.0 tools give you the ability to reach out to new and existing users, increasing your ability to reach the Long Tail of users, a primary goal of Library 2.0. (We looked at this goal more in-depth in Chapter 5.)

The list of tools discussed in this section is not exhaustive; many other Web 2.0 tools exist, and new ones are being introduced almost daily. A quick look at the TechCrunch blog (www.techcrunch.com) will convince you that bright programmers are writing new applications almost faster than anyone can review them. But the tools discussed here lie at the heart of many services libraries will want to offer, both internally, to our staff, and externally, to our users.

Blogs—Internal

Internal blogs are those that are made available only to people within the organization. The public should not have ready access to this type of blog; instead, it should be used as a method of communication among library staff. Blogs that are external, or made available to the public, are discussed later in this chapter.

Branch, Department, or Local Level Blogging

New staffing models, changes in staffing levels and operating hours, and the hectic day-to-day work every librarian faces make communications difficult. Branch staff don't seem to have the time they once did to talk to each other about the difficulties they face or the coping skills they learn. Management has an increasingly difficult time getting together with staff for face-to-face meetings. This opportunity for communication that we seem to be losing, though, is vital to our libraries. Whereas at one time staff members would arrive in the morning and have the time to discuss library happenings with one another, today's work pace often does not allow for that camaraderie. The social interaction that underpinned the sense of family within the library is now, more often than not, missing.

Efficiency has displaced the sense of team. Yet, because we are human, we need social interaction—even, or perhaps especially, at work. Every day, we spend approximately nine hours with our co-workers. Yes, we must get the work of the day accomplished, but we also need to be able to communicate the things that are important to us, share with our fellow workers the happenings in our lives, and share our workplace concerns in a receptive environment. As providers of direct customer service we need the kind of environment that allows us to blow off steam, talk in an open and honest atmosphere, and prepare ourselves in a team-like manner for the trials of the day. Interacting with customers every day, all day, can be exhausting, further limiting our energy for the internal communication that is so critical. The reality of our lives now is such that we may never again have that much "down time" at the beginning of each workday. We may not be able to spend time commiserating in the break room as often as we would like. Therefore, we need to find a tool that will to some extent allow this type of communication to continue. Staff members need a way to talk to fellow staff, and management needs a way to talk with frontline staff.

One tool that works exceptionally well at facilitating both types of communication is a blog. A simple blog created with software such as Blogger (www.blogger.com), WordPress (www.wordpress.org), or Movable Type (www.sixapart.com/movabletype) can accomplish several important things for branch staff. First, blog communication is asynchronous. You do not have to get people together at the same time as you do for chat or face-to-face meetings. Local or branch blogs also enable horizontal communication among staff members. You can replicate the break room, help desk, and circulation room discussions right there on the blog. Morning crews can talk to night crews about new procedures without always having to try to find 15 minutes to break away at the same time. Staff members who rarely cross paths at work, such as those who work on opposite shifts, can discuss work-related topics, such as new materials, policy or procedure questions, library happenings, or programming and outreach events—all while the ideas and thoughts are fresh in their minds. The amount of information that can be shared across this medium is endless.

Internal blogs also facilitate vertical communications, letting management talk with frontline staff. Here, there can be several advantages to the communal concept of blogs, provided that management encourages an open and welcoming blogging atmosphere. Staff can pose questions or concerns in the department or branch blog community; these postings will receive attention and feedback from fellow staff. Management will be curious to see what staff members are writing but also should be expected to participate as needed. Managers must expeditiously provide a credible and reasonable response to any posted question. If a staff person, for example, complains about feeling insecure in the building when the local school lets out and more than 100 teens come pouring into the building, then it is incumbent upon his manager to respond in a timely and honest manner. If she delays in responding, or if her answer is political instead of honest and pragmatic, then her credibility as a leader will diminish and staff will develop an unfavorable attitude toward the blog.

To get the most out of this (or any internal blog), staff and managers must be sure to maintain professionalism in their postings and comments. Posted questions and answers should be presented in a professional and courteous, though not necessarily formal, manner. Otherwise, the atmosphere of the blog could turn hostile, and staff and managers would be at risk for creating a tense work environment. While the blog is a great form of open communication, it is not an excuse or outlet for irresponsible or outrageous behavior.

This example of a department or branch blog is easily expanded to a system-wide tool, but there is much to be said for keeping this type of blog central to one local community within a larger organization. Branch and department blogs differ from system-wide blogs. System-wide blogs, as discussed in the next section, are a great means for directors and top-level management to interact with librarians and support staff. This direct connection provides a communications link that can be beneficial whenever the need arises to share information to all staff quickly. But in medium to large library systems, a system-wide blog may not be the best place for staff members to interact with each other on a regular basis—if only because of the level of chatter that may result from several hundred staff using the same communications tool. Branch and department blogs can effectively carry the local traffic, while the system blog is reserved for big-picture discussions and director-to-staff vertical communications.

Top-Down Blogging

Just as it is important for the staff within a local building or community to be able to communicate with management, so it is important for the entire system to hear from the top-level administration. Administrators often underestimate the power of their words when it comes to workplace morale. Administrators speak with so many people every day, but they rarely get the opportunity to speak directly with the librarians and support staff in each department or branch. Practically, it is impossible to expect library directors to go out and regularly visit every branch, sit and talk with every employee, and still be able to get the rest of their work accomplished. Administrators are not nine-to-five employees. They take their jobs home and with them on vacation; they spend each day balancing the many scheduled items on their calendars with the inevitable crises and emergencies that are bound to arise every day.

Many administrators and directors make the mistake of assuming that the rest of the library staff knows just how hard they are working. The reality, though, is that staff are so busy doing their own jobs that they often do not see or hear what their administrators are doing. Quite often, staff members have no idea that the issues they feel are important are also important to and being addressed by the library administration. Management and administration seem to do a poor job of relaying to staff just what they are working on. Morale begins to suffer when staff feel that their concerns are not shared by their leadership.

Here, a simple blog can play a very important role in improving vertical communications. The key in an example like this is to create buy-in with the library leadership. The director should write a blog entry every week—one or two paragraphs about the most important or exciting issues facing the library. Soon, staff will begin reading and commenting. If the director takes the time to respond to staff comments, even better. A two-way dialogue between top leadership and their branch and department staff is essential. Even if the director cannot respond to each individual comment, then perhaps her next entry can begin with a broad response to all comments received during the previous week.

The key here is not to encourage a detailed and laborious dialogue between the director and staff; it is merely for staff to hear from the director directly and to know that she has an understanding of the important issues they deal with daily. The goal is for staff to know that their concerns are the director's concerns, and that the issues staff are talking and worrying about are being addressed by the director. The director's blog entries don't even have to have concrete solutions to every issue; they just need to discuss these issues. The benefits that directors can reap from such communication, by letting their workers know that they share their worries and that they are working toward solutions, are immense—certainly worth the 10 or 20 minutes a week that it takes to write a simple blog post.

Blogs—External

What the blog can do for internal communication, it can also do for external communication. External blogs are open to your community of users, providing information and often inviting participation and feedback. By following the same model as with its internal blogs, any library can create both a single, top-level, system blog that allows for

Blog Applications

There are two primary ways of setting up a blog. The first is to use an online Web-based application such as Blogger (www.blogger.com) and let this company serve as the host for your blog. This is by far the easiest way to begin blogging, as it requires no technical skills and is very simple to set up and use. Some services, like Blogger, are free. Others, like TypePad (www.typepad.com), charge monthly fees. Web sites providing easy-to-use hosted online blogging include:

- Blogger, www.blogger.com
- LiveJournal, www.livejournal.com
- WordPress.com, www.wordpress.com
- TypePad, www.typepad.com
- Xanga, www.xanga.com

(Note that LiveJournal and Xanga are more heavily used by a younger demographic and may be viewed as less "professional" than the other services.)

A more complex, but ultimately more flexible, way of setting up your blog involves downloading blogging software and installing it on your own server (or through your own contracted service). You'll find both open-source and proprietary blogging software. These packages include:

- Drupal, www.drupal.org
- Movable Type, www.sixapart.com/movabletype
- WordPress, www.wordpress.org

general communication between the director and library customers and more specific blogs for narrower, focused discussions between library staff and customers.

Broad purpose front-page blogs serve as your library's first point of contact with library customers online. Instead of simply pushing one-way content to them via announcements or calendars, we can now post this information and accept comments and questions in response. As librarians, we know that a give-and-take conversation is critical to being understood. We work with the reference interview every day; the give and take of a dialogue can make conversations clearer and more easily understood. With blogs, when a question comes through, it no longer lives in seclusion—and its answer is not just for one person, but becomes available to all visitors.

When we publish information about an upcoming library event or service and receive a question concerning this information on our new blog, the response we post to that question will be available to the entire community. Librarians know that for every person who asks where a section or particular item is located in the library, there are five to 10 more people who did not take the time to query or were afraid to ask. Now, extrapolate this to our Web sites. How many questions regarding our services go unasked? How many people will each question represent? When you begin looking at communications in this manner, you can more easily justify the expense and time in setting up an external blog.

An excellent example of a top-level blog can be found on the Ann Arbor District Library's Web page (www.aadl.org), which was honored by the ALA in 2006 as the "best Web site" for libraries with budgets of $6 million or more (see Figure 5.2 in Chapter 5). Its Web site effectively integrates a blog into the library's main Web page by using Drupal, an open-source content management software. AADL's Web services staff crafted the blog so that it unobtrusively allows for direct customer interaction right on the first page every visitor sees. (See more on AADL's site in Chapter 5.)

One of the great advantages of using a blog to communicate with your customers is the ability to use RSS (really simple syndication) feeds. Customers can subscribe to your RSS feed and receive updates as you publish them, so that they can be notified of new information or content without having to actually remember to revisit your Web page. For instance, let's say that you set up a blog about your teen activities. As with almost all blogging software, an RSS feed is automatically generated. Your users subscribe to this feed using any number of free aggregators such as Bloglines (www.bloglines.com) or Netvibes (www.netvibes.com). This way, when you publish new content on your blog, your users get this information "pushed" to them via their RSS aggregator. It's like having a direct line to your customers.

More focused external blogs can be utilized in a plethora of ways, such as for book clubs, teen groups, and students. External blogs can be open or invite-only. They can be stand-alone blogs, or they can be integrated into the online catalog through links from specific titles. They can also be connected to keyword searches. Imagine entering "sewing" as a keyword search and finding not only books on sewing, but a blog on the subject that is administered by the sewing club that meets every Thursday at your local branch. This type of mashup, or merging of two distinct applications (in this case, the catalog and the blog), is but one of the many possibilities available to libraries when examining 2.0 technologies.

Wikis and Knowledge Management—Internal

Have you ever been to a retirement party where someone asked a question like, "What are we going to do without [the person retiring]?" Some department head or manager or specialized taskmaster retires, and suddenly no one has the slightest clue how that person did his job. It turns out that, even though he was there for years, working diligently and turning out high-quality work day after day, none of the knowledge he amassed over those years was saved. When this person is replaced, days and weeks pass unproductively as some poor schmuck struggles to piece together the puzzle that is his new job.

At least with the previous scenario, you have some warning. Once a person announces his retirement, you can scramble to gather and save as much of his accumulated information as possible. But, imagine that you have a multimillion-dollar project in the works, and the primary project manager suddenly falls ill and goes on extended leave. Here you are, committed to multiple vendors, hip-deep in complicated plans and complex communications between private and government entities, and you are stranded with nothing to help you figure it all out: no written plans, no timeline of whom to contact and when. This is the sort of catastrophe that can bring down an administration.

Unfortunately, this type of thing happens far too often and not only in libraries. But the fact that it does happen in libraries is frustrating, because we are supposed to be so good at capturing and organizing knowledge. We are the organizers, the catalogers, the managers of information. But when it comes to what we do in our daily jobs, our hard-won internal operating information seems to take a backseat to our external customer service.

Yet, if we want to do more with less and serve more with the same—or less—then we need to improve the way we capture our knowledge. We cannot allow ourselves to become dependent on one individual's personally held knowledge. We need to get that information down in writing, and one excellent way to accomplish this is through the use of a wiki, a Web site that allows users to easily edit and add content. (Anyone who has made use of Wikipedia has a basic understanding of the way a wiki works.) The wiki provides us with a tool of amazing power. As an internal tool, the wiki has many advantages over a simple system based on documents and files. First, it allows for community collaboration. Entire departments can contribute to the wiki, which means, for example, that every IT technician can record every trouble-ticket they work on. This, in turn, builds a knowledgebase that other technicians can then draw upon. Wikis also provide for a clear revision history. This means that every time a wiki entry is changed, that change is recorded and the previous version is archived, creating an electronic paper trail.

Getting staff to contribute to the wiki should only be as hard as convincing them that the benefits to all far outweigh the initial time involved. The amount of staff time saved in the long run will be well worth the upfront efforts required. To again use IT as an example, imagine how many times staff have sent in trouble-tickets on issues that they could easily fix on their own without having to wait on the busy IT department—if they had the information necessary to show them how to proceed. Now, imagine having instructions on how to correct easily fixed PC issues accessible on a wiki that staff can search. Self-sufficiency is not just for our external customers!

Wiki Applications

Much as with blogging software, you can find both online, developer-hosted wikis (often called wiki farms) and downloadable wiki software that you install on your own server or upload to your own contracted hosting service. There are also both open-source and proprietary versions of downloadable software. All of the wiki providers listed here offer at least a basic free version, in addition to a more complex paid version.

Some popular wiki farms include:

- Wikia, www.wikia.com/wiki/Wikia
- JotSpot, www.jotspot.com
- PBwiki, www.pbwiki.com
- SeedWiki, www.seedwiki.com
- Wikispaces, www.wikispaces.com

Downloadable wiki software includes:

- MediaWiki, www.mediawiki.org
- TWiki, www.twiki.org
- XWiki, www.xwiki.org

Wikis and Knowledge Management—External

All of the benefits of the internal wiki apply to an external one, with the added benefit of it being accessible to many, many more people. The strength of a wiki is directly proportional to its number of contributors. Much like blogs, wikis help us capture our community's knowledge and collect it in a manageable way, making it accessible to everyone. Wikis are more than simple encyclopedic databases; they can be a place for discussion. (Take a look at almost any article in Wikipedia and click on the "discussion" tab for an example.) Wikis can also be a repository for documents and multimedia content. They can be as simple or as complex as needed, as demonstrated by the Saint Joseph County Public Library's (SJCPL) Subject Guides wiki project (www.libraryforlife.org/subjectguides/index.php/Main_Page). The SJCPL wiki originally was created by librarians but is now open to customer comments.

There are numerous examples of ways to use wikis to reach users. Want to reach out to local genealogy aficionados? Try setting up a genealogy wiki, and see how many people join in the first month. The wiki is ideally suited to genealogical knowledge management, and if you choose an easy-to-use wiki with a WYSIWYG (what you see is what you get) interface, you will likely be very pleased with its success. Wikis also provide an excellent place for interest groups to archive their knowledge. Local Little League baseball statisticians, political junkies, scholarly religious groups, or any other type of community group could benefit from a subject-specific wiki. Toss in a blog for them to discuss current issues, and you may quickly create a very happy and tech-savvy group of library users.

Interview with Meredith Farkas, Distance Learning Librarian

We asked Meredith Farkas, distance learning librarian at Norwich University in Vermont, for her take on wikis and social networking.

Starting a wiki project requires staff participation, which can be difficult at the beginning. How can a library motivate staff to play an active role?

It can be very difficult to ensure staff buy-in with wiki projects, especially if the majority of staff bristles at the idea of learning a new technology. There are a number of things you can do to make this easier. The first is to choose a wiki that is incredibly easy to use. Many of the wiki software options are moving toward being WYSIWYG, which would prevent your users from having to learn complicated wiki markup. The second thing you can do is to get enthusiastic support from above, which is critical to communicating to staff that this is a project they need to pay attention to. Third, you should seed the wiki, both with content and with lots of documentation. No one will use a wiki that is a blank slate and that lacks any instructions on its use. Fourth, offer wiki trainings and make them fun. Mary Carmen Chimato at SUNY Stony Brook's Health Sciences Library bought decorations and had a Hawaiian-themed wiki party/training for each separate unit at the library. Finally, keep the wiki on people's radar. Don't just assume that training will be enough. Keep reminding people about the wiki and how they can use it to make their lives easier.

In what ways do you see social networks improving library outreach?

Many libraries have started building presence in MySpace and Facebook by creating profiles. There are two ways that libraries can use social networks to provide valuable outreach services. The first is by using the profile as a two-way communications mechanism. Libraries can capitalize on the "Comments" area in MySpace or on "The Wall" in Facebook. By asking patrons questions in a space where they feel safe enough to express themselves, libraries could get valuable feedback from their patrons about library services and materials. The second method of providing outreach through social networks is by using the profile as a portal to the library Web site and services. Some libraries have made their Facebook or MySpace site an extension of the library Web site, with links to the catalog, chat reference pages, research guides, calendars of events, and more. If students are largely spending their time in MySpace and Facebook, putting links to library services on these sites just makes it that much easier for them to access the library.

Instant Messaging and Chat—Internal

Instant messaging (IM) and chat tools provide for multiparticipant synchronous discussions across broad distances. There are numerous IM and chat applications available, including ones that run entirely through the Web browser and require no local software installation. These applications can be useful for internal branch communications, for example, when team members are spread across geographically diverse branches or departments. Individuals can work together on their assigned project via chat or IM. When numerous individuals are working different shifts in different locations, all dealing with local variations of the team's project, communicating via e-mail or face-to-face meetings can be messy and difficult to schedule.

Instant Messaging and Chat Applications

Instant messaging clients come in several flavors. Most of the major IM services offer software that only speaks to people using the same service, though this has started to change, with Yahoo! Messenger and Windows Messenger now offering cross-service interoperability. IM provider software is available for download from:

- AOL Instant Messenger (AIM), www.aim.com
- Yahoo! Messenger, messenger.yahoo.com
- Windows Live Messenger, messenger.msn.com
- Google Talk, www.google.com/talk

Another class of IM software allows you to message across multiple services. This type of software is called an IM aggregator or multiprotocol client, and is available from:

- Trillian (for PC), www.ceruleanstudios.com
- Fire (for Mac), fire.sourceforge.net
- Gaim, gaim.sourceforge.net

Finally, a few browser-based IM applications require no download at all, running from inside your Web browser. These services include:

- meebo, www.meebo.com
- goowy, www.goowy.com
- Google Talk (from within Gmail), mail.google.com

An application like Zoho Chat (zohochat.com) or 37 Signals'
Campfire (www.campfirenow.com) can serve as an excellent tool for
bringing together a diverse group of staff under one virtual roof.
Applications like Zoho Chat allow the team leader to schedule meetings
and send invitations, negating the need for each individual to sign up
and register for the service. This is beneficial, as it is important to put
up as few obstacles as possible when dealing with large and techno-
logically diverse groups.

Instant Messaging and Chat—External

Instant messaging reference, or IM Help, is a natural follow-on to
the e-mail and telephone reference so many libraries have been providing. With more than 62 percent of Generation Y currently using IM,
your library can extend its reach into this difficult-to-target demographic. Creating and promoting an IM service requires little in the
way of software or computer costs, but does require training and planning. According to the PEW report *How Americans Use Instant
Messaging*, as of September 2004, there were 53 million IM users in
the U.S. Of those 53 million, a full 24 percent reported using IM *more*
frequently than e-mail. As would be expected, younger Internet users
utilize IM at a far greater rate than older Internet users. Within the
18–27 age group (Generation Y), 57 percent report using IM more frequently than e-mail. Interestingly, the PEW survey showed that women
IM users, as a group, spend far more time online than men.[2]

It should come as no surprise that IM users are the group most comfortable with computers and electronic information. Users of IM multitask; 32 percent say they *always* multitask! Reaching out to this
demographic should be a top priority, and IM Help is one easy way to
do just that. By putting ourselves out there amid teens and young
adults, we will be better positioned to bring the library to our users,
instead of always trying to bring our users to the library. Providing this
service is not technically complicated, although there are numerous
policy and philosophical questions that will need to be addressed; you

will also need to provide training. Library Success, a wiki dedicated to library best practices, has an excellent entry on setting up IM Help (www.libsuccess.org/index.php?title=Online_Reference).

IM Help has the potential to reach out and grab a user base that may not yet take advantage of your library. For public libraries, heavy marketing to school-age and young adult populations can boost the success of the service. Reach out to the schools in your area, visiting middle and high schools when possible. College libraries should market to the entire student body, as many of them likely use IM on a daily basis (Figure 6.1). Make business cards with your library's IM service prominently displayed. Hand them out to teens in the library, put them in young adult books on hold, pass them out to the college students around campus, and make sure every outreach librarian takes some with them wherever they go.

Podcasting

Podcasting is all about the push. Anyone can record an MP3 file of a storytime or author presentation, post it to a Web site, and wait for

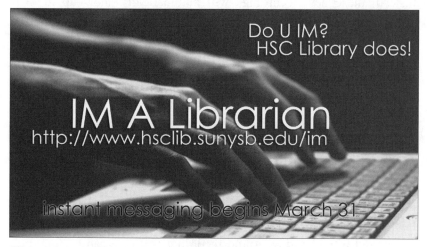

Figure 6.1   IM poster for the Health Sciences Center Library at Stony Brook University (designed by Darren Chase, photo by Brian Adison).

people to come and get it. But this is a book about 2.0, and in 2.0, we don't sit back and wait for anything! Podcasting is all about the push— the RSS push, that is. Podcasting is very easy to do and can offer a very big return on what is often a minimal investment. With a podcast or a video podcast, you create and publish audio or video content and your users subscribe to it just as they would subscribe to a magazine or newspaper.

Without getting too technical, the RSS component of the podcast is what gets your library's sound recording (or video) to your users' computer, or to their iPod or other mobile device. It is important to remember that you can listen to these podcasts on far more than just headphones plugged into a tiny MP3 player. Dad can play the new recording from the home computer, letting the kids sit and eat lunch while listening to the library's production of The Three Bears, and Mom can listen to last night's author interview while balancing her checking account. By subscribing to your podcast, your users will be assured of always getting updates when new recordings are released. Library users don't have to continually check back to the programming page of your Web site to see if any new stories have been released. Instead, these new recordings will automatically show up in their iTunes (www.apple.com/itunes) or similar service. Your users have many choices when it comes to applications designed to subscribe to podcasts; one popular and easy-to-use choice is iTunes, for both Windows and Apple.

Getting started with podcasting is very simple. Numerous MP3 recording devices are available, though you really do not even need one of those if you want to be super-efficient and use your computer as the recorder. However, if you want the broadcast to really sound good, it may be worth the investment to purchase a digital voice recorder and a microphone. The Podcasters Wiki (www.podcasterswiki.com) maintains a list of devices and software, along with helpful hints on how to get started in podcasting. Audio recording software can be found on most Windows (Sound Recorder) and Apple (GarageBand) computers. One powerful, free, and open-source tool is Audacity (audacity.source forge.net). Audacity allows you to record live audio and then cut, copy, splice, and mix it before converting it to MP3 format.

You'll find there are numerous services that can be podcasted out to your community. Storytimes and author or celebrity visits can be audio recorded—just be sure to talk to the author's agent beforehand, and work the podcast into the contract. Puppet shows and magic shows can be video recorded using a simple digital video recorder or Webcam, and pushed out to users in the same manner. Board meetings and other open meetings can also be recorded for your users. Once you start brainstorming, the possibilities will seem endless. Almost every outreach event or program can be used over and over again, reaching more users than ever before, thanks to podcasting. No longer should we practice for and put on a program, only to see bad weather or poorly timed scheduling limit our audience. From now on, we should view every program as an event that can be recorded and shown again time after time to users who can watch them where and when they want. Look around and check out what other libraries that are using this technology are doing. Lansing (IL) Public Library (www.lansing.lib.il.us) is an excellent example of a library using podcasts (and blogs) to reach out to teens and adults.

Social Networking

Social networking is another offshoot of Web 2.0 that libraries are beginning to explore and put to use. Numerous social networks have sprouted in recent years, and it has become a multibillion-dollar industry with millions of daily users. To understand the popularity and worth of such services, just look at the short history of MySpace (www.myspace.com). MySpace was founded in July 2003 by Tom Anderson and Chris DeWolfe, and gained almost instant popularity as a teen hangout. Ask any teen today, and they will tell you MySpace is the place to be. Since MySpace has an estimated user base of more than 100 million, you should not have to look very far to find a MySpace fan.

Numbers like this are astounding, and it is no surprise that many libraries have started looking at MySpace and other social networking sites as places to reach out to our community of library users and potential users. An excellent example of a library's MySpace presence is the "Freedom Teen Zone" from the Freedom Regional Public Library of the Public Library of Charlotte & Mecklenburg County (NC) (www.myspace.com/freedomteenzone). This well-designed MySpace site includes a calendar of library events that appeal to teens (Figure 6.2).

The Public Library of Charlotte & Mecklenburg County has also created the MySpace page "The Loft @ ImaginOn" (www.myspace. com/libraryloft). Here, the library takes the added measure of providing a page attempting to educate teens on the safe use of social networks. Titled "Social Networking Sites: Safety Tips for Teens," the page states:

> You've probably learned a long list of important safety and privacy lessons already: Look both ways before crossing the street; buckle up; hide your diary where your nosy brother can't find it; don't talk to strangers.
>
> The Federal Trade Commission, the nation's consumer protection agency, is urging kids to add one more lesson to the list: Don't post information about yourself online that you don't want the whole world to know. The Internet is the world's biggest information exchange: Many more people could see your information than you intend, including your parents, your teachers, your employer, the police and strangers, some of whom could be dangerous.
>
> Social networking sites have added a new factor to the friends of friends equation. By providing information about yourself and using blogs, chat rooms, e-mail, or instant messaging, you can communicate, either within a limited community, or with the world at large. But while the sites can increase your circle of friends, they also can increase

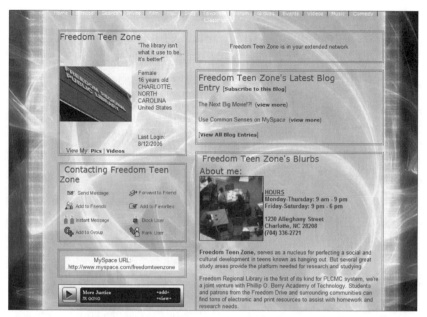

Figure 6.2   "Freedom Teen Zone" on MySpace from the Freedom
Regional Public Library of the Public Library of Charlotte
& Mecklenburg County.

your exposure to people who have less-than-friendly inten-
tions. You've heard the stories about people who were
stalked by someone they met online, had their identity
stolen, or had their computer hacked.

Hennepin County (MN) Public Library also has created a page on
MySpace (www.myspace.com/hennepincountylibrary). The library
maintains a very attractive MySpace presence—with the humorous
twist of identifying itself as an 86-year-old female (Figure 6.3).

Although it's the largest social networking site, MySpace is by no
means the only one. Facebook (www.facebook.com), aimed at a
slightly older customer than MySpace, claims a very large share of the
college-age social network user base. Friendster (www.friendster.com)
serves yet a slightly older demographic, targeting young adults in their
20s and 30s.

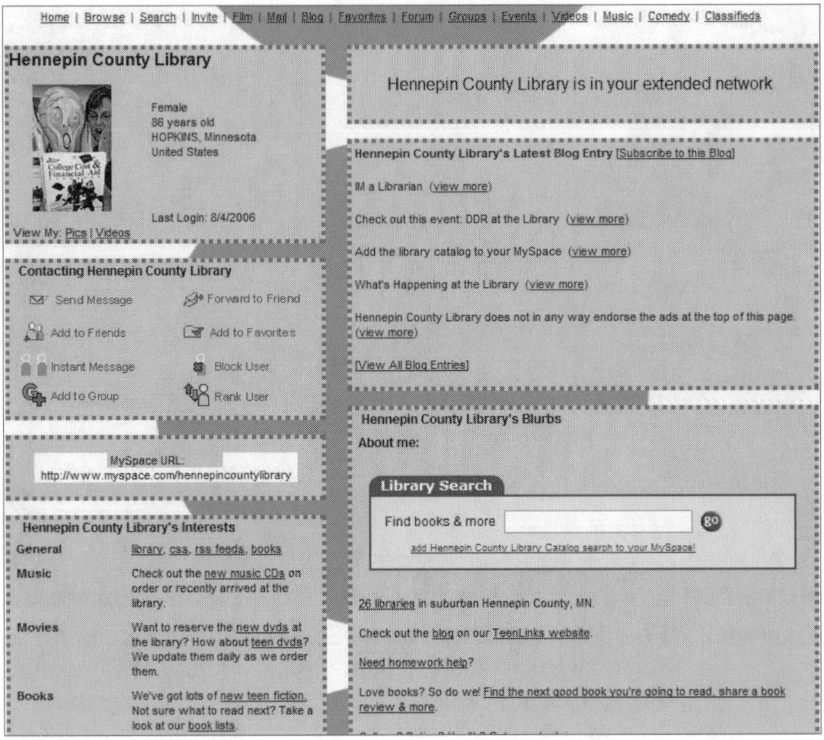

Figure 6.3   Hennepin County Public Library's MySpace page.

Flickr (www.flickr.com) is a popular online photo sharing network, with many libraries using the service to reach out to their communities, both local and professional, with images of new buildings, services, and events. The Bloomington (IL) Public Library (www.flickr.com/photos/bloomingtonlibrary) maintains a Flickr account that had more than 1,000 images as of December 2006 (Figure 6.4). Along with Bloomington Public Library, more than 30 other public, academic, and special libraries maintain Flickr accounts. Most libraries post photos of programming and events, but many also post behind-the-scenes images of building projects, staff parties and retreats, and other activities the public would not normally have a way to see. By getting their images "out there," libraries are better able to become a part of the community, appealing, as Michael Stephens wrote on his Tame the Web blog, to the heart and "put[ting] humanity into the library's virtual presence."[3]

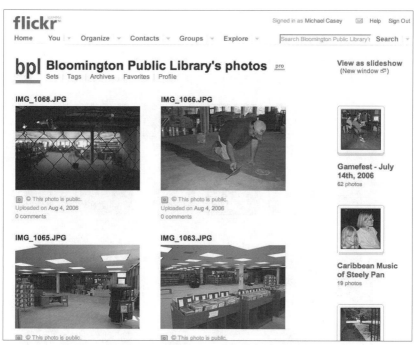

Figure 6.4   Bloomington Public Library's Flickr page.

Librarians are also using Flickr to meet other librarians and share photos. Started by Michael Porter, the Flickr group "Libraries and Librarians" (www.flickr.com/groups/librariesandlibrarians) boasted more than 1,000 members and more than 7,000 photographs as of August 2006 (Figure 6.5). Librarians submit photos of their own branches, libraries they visit while traveling, photos from conferences, and just about anything else library related.

Steven M. Cohen's Flickr group "Librarian Trading Cards" (www.flickr.com/groups/librariancards) had more than 300 members as of December 2006 and a unique collection of images (Figure 6.6). The project was started by Amy Pelman on her blog, Librarian Trading Cards (librariantradingcards.blogspot.com). This group makes classic trading cards depicting themselves and their favorite librarians in a fun, humorous way.

Figure 6.5   The Libraries and Librarians group on Flickr.

Getting "out there" and participating in social networks is not an easy decision for many libraries to make. Social networks such as MySpace are primarily the domain of teens, and teens and libraries sometimes have a difficult time getting along. MySpace also reflects the reality of teen life, with flashy Web pages overflowing with music, videos, and sometimes risqué images. MySpace is the virtual version of the corner gathering place, combined with the forwardness and daring of a teen hangout. But MySpace is where the teens are, and any library brave enough to enter has the chance of coming away with new users in a difficult to capture demographic.

The choice to get "out there" is sometimes politically difficult. Social networks have a strained relationship with libraries. Parents

Figure 6.6   The Librarian Trading Cards group on Flickr.

fear for their children's safety on MySpace and other popular social networks. Media reports tend to increase the negative attention being paid to such Web sites. Recent federal government efforts to restrict access to social networks in libraries and schools, including the Deleting Online Predators Act (DOPA, H.R. 5319), make for an uncertain future for the use of social networks in libraries. It is our responsibility to educate our customers, staff, governing board, local community leaders, and politicians about social networks and their role in library service. Be prepared to demonstrate the uses of social networks and point out their positive contribution to our communities and to our ability to provide customer-driven services. What this ultimately comes down to is serving your community within the limits imposed on you. As with all services, take into consideration the needs of your particular community of users when deciding to participate in online social networks such as MySpace.

ENDNOTES

1. Michael Stephens, "Technoplans vs. Technolust," *Library Journal*, November 1, 2004, www.libraryjournal.com/article/CA474999.html.

2. Eulynn Shiu and Amanda Lenhart, "How Americans Use Instant Messaging," *PEW Report*, August 31, 2004, www.pewinternet.org/PPF/r/133/report_display.asp: i, iii, 3, 11, 16.

3. Michael Stephens, "Top Ten Techie Things for Librarians 2006 (Updated)," Tame the Web, tametheweb.com/2006/01/ten_techie_things_for_libraria _1.html.

7

Buy-In: Getting Everyone on Board

"As much as an administrator wants a change, it will never effectively happen if staff do not buy into it."
—Michael A. Golrick

This chapter discusses possibly the most important element in implementing Library 2.0: staff and customer buy-in. The following sections address the importance of drawing an honest picture for everyone involved, of both the current state of your library and where you want to go. Here you'll read about ways to sell change to and encourage collaboration between your community and your organization, as well as among the different levels of your organization, including the governing board, administration, and staff. You'll also learn tips for dealing with the dreaded (but likely unavoidable) Reluctant Person or Department—or, those who resist change. Finally, we provide information on ways to continually promote Library 2.0 in your organization, to encourage ongoing buy-in.

A fundamental system-wide change to library operations cannot succeed unless both staff and administration are on board. Strategies for obtaining staff buy-in are similar to those used through Library 2.0 for sustaining and satisfying your library users. Specifically, in the process of creating and implementing any solution, we must always include the very people who will use and be responsible for that service.

Collaborative participation will create goodwill and keep your staff and administrators informed of the process.

DRAWING AN HONEST PICTURE

Before we can create the environment of collaborative participation between library staff and administrators that lets us successfully enact change, we must provide all involved parties with a clear picture of where we are now—and of where we want to go. We must describe the current state of our library or department, and identify what needs to be improved or accomplished to make the proposed changes work.

Think back to Chapter 3, where we discussed the importance of figuring out where your library is now before you can move on to Library 2.0. You should use the data discussed in that chapter to help draw an honest picture of the current state of your library. There are many ways to present this information. If your library already creates an annual report that evaluates the state of the organization, it will likely contain the data you need. You can also compile this information into an informal report, using data sheets about your library you already have handy, such as spreadsheets of collection usage over the year or a written community analysis. Either way, begin by gathering a packet of information that assesses your library's current situation, which you will need to understand before you can determine how your library can work toward Library 2.0. Having a clear picture of the current state of your library will also assist you with encouraging participation and buy-in for changes and Library 2.0 within your organization. How successful is your library or department now? You will want to consider both hard and soft statistics. Are circulation numbers up or down? What about the number of reference transactions? And door count? How is your event attendance? And what about Web site visits? How much use are your databases getting? These are questions that need to be answered.

Also consider any circumstances that may contribute to the rise or fall of these numbers. For example, if all of your library's public computers default to the library's main Web page with each new session, you will need to account for this when analyzing Web site use statistics. In a case like this, you would also want to consider the effects of having a visually appealing, user-friendly, and extremely functional library Web page as the first thing customers see when logging onto a public computer. This is particularly important, because your library's Web page is the window dressing and advertisement for your library and the services you provide. Do you have a method for customers and staff to provide feedback on the Web page and library catalog? If so (and we really hope you do!), evaluate this user feedback as well as your responses when designing a user-friendly Web site. Much of your success depends not only on the usefulness of your collection and staff but also on the functionality of your library's Web site. Your library's Web site should be viewed as an online extension of your physical library.

You will also want to take into account customer and staff feedback on library collections, buildings, services, and events. Does your library have an outlet for customers and staff to make suggestions, such as through a paper or electronic form? If so, a compiled list of these comments should also be considered when evaluating the current state of the library. A recent community analysis, if available, can also be included in your evaluation. Consider the impact of changes in your community, such as an increase in homelessness or the opening of a new local high school. To paint a clear picture, you must reflect on the bad as well as the good. Does your library have a method for reporting incidents, such as vandalism or injuries? These can also provide telling feedback about what your staff faces on a daily basis. Hiding negatives will only hinder your ability to realistically evaluate your library's success. Without a clear picture of where you are now, your library lacks direction as it tries to move forward, and you will have difficulty getting everyone on board.

Once you have compiled all of your data and created a thorough library analysis, formally or informally, you should think about what needs to be improved. If you have critically evaluated both your statistics and customer and staff feedback, areas that need adjustment should be fairly obvious. If you see several areas that need to be improved, go ahead and list them all, but be prepared to focus on just a few areas to begin with. When trying to get everyone on board, you will need to have a well thought-out plan that will not overwhelm staff or administrators. After starting small, by focusing on just a few areas and obtaining buy-in, you ultimately will be able to achieve improvements to all of the areas that need developing.

One way to determine your initial areas of focus is through reviewing your library or department's strategic plan. If one of your library's strategic plan goals is to increase teen appeal, and an area that needs improvement is teen attendance, then service to teens would likely be a good place to start. Much as a library creates goals for its strategic plan, you will want to set high goals for improvement—but also be realistic. It is important to both think big and stay grounded, which can be a difficult task. Your ideas for change and improvement will need to be rational in order to obtain staff and administrator buy-in.

You will also want to consider the tools that you will need to accomplish your goals. The essential ingredients of Library 2.0 listed in Chapter 2 can help you determine the tools you will need to incorporate Library 2.0 into your organization. Also, think back to the technologies discussed in Chapter 6. What free or affordable technologies can help you enact change and meet your goals for improvement? Success is based on an effective use of many tools, not just a few; you will not want to fixate on any one new tool as a magic wand to resolve all of your problems. Rather, think about how several tools can work together to help you accomplish your big-picture goals.

You will not be able to approach staff, administrators, or your governing board with a plan for working toward Library 2.0 until you have created an honest picture of where your library is now and the improvements the library should make. Once you form a clear picture, you will feel confident in your approach.

DISCUSSING CHANGE

Many people find change intimidating. You are likely to experience resistance from some staff members, particularly when discussing change of such magnitude that it will have a system-wide effect. When you first introduce your ideas for change, you will be wise to directly address the aspects of change that are likely to create the most apprehension in those you wish to sell it to. Most staff will primarily be concerned with how the change will affect them personally, while you will need to convince your administrators and governing board of the return on investment and how this change will help the organization accomplish both its short-term and long-term goals.

When selling change, your initial approach should stress the importance of preserving and meeting the mission of the library. By this point, you should at least have determined what general initial changes need to be made, and it is crucial that these changes fulfill the mission of the library. If they work against this mission, they will be nearly impossible to sell to your board, administrators, staff, and customers. Knowing whether your ideas for change fit the goals of your organization will require that you have a very clear understanding of the library's mission. If your library does not have a clearly defined mission statement, you will need to determine the library's purpose. What is the perceived role of the library within its community, to staff, to the governing board, and to the community you serve? As long as everyone agrees on the mission, differences of opinions and different desires on changes to services are acceptable; in fact, you will find this often to be the case. However, all parties involved must come to a consensus on the library's long-term goals. The services will change, but the mission should not.

Although preserving the library's mission is imperative, when seeking buy-in, it is equally important that your proposal stress the fluidity of change itself. Whatever does not work will again be changed or adjusted. You build on your successes, not your failures. Make everyone involved aware that, if a service, task, or idea fails to work as anticipated—or could be improved—it will be addressed. Nothing is constant. Explain the procedure for updates and evaluations of the change. Let people know that changes will be appraised on a regularly scheduled basis, and that the library will track progress to ensure that all long-term goals are met.

Most importantly, be sure to include in every discussion about change the point that the organization does not intend to change things simply for the sake of change. Any changes or updates to services or procedures need to reflect the current needs of the community served and of the organization as a whole. Change can be scary, but when staff and customers are well informed about an impending change, the reasons behind it, and the benefits stemming from it, you will see a more positive reaction. The phrase "constant change," in particular, can be intimidating to those who are unsure about what this entails. If not clearly explained, constant change can easily be assumed to mean that change will happen willy-nilly, just to be sure it is constant. Library 2.0, however, is not achieved through change for the sake of change; change is always a necessary step toward improving library services and operations.

When discussing the method of constant change your organization will adopt, you also will want to clarify that the change will apply to all services, procedures, and library operations. As one librarian told us: "There are times when I think we change for the sake of changing, and there are some processes that are so horribly entrenched in years of 'we've always done it this way' that they'll never budge." Much as you want to avoid unnecessary changes, you also want to avoid cases in which the only changes that occur are handpicked by the library's administration.

One benefit of constant change is that your staff and customers will soon be well aware of the frequent updates in services. The important thing to remember is that the purpose of the "constant" element in this type of change is not to constantly throw people off guard, as is often assumed. Instead, its purpose is to constantly evaluate and consider updating services and procedures in order to make them better for your users, as well as for your staff. Refer to Chapter 4 for more information on creating an environment of constant, purposeful change.

SELLING TO DIFFERENT LEVELS

Governing Board

Of main interest to most governing boards will be satisfying the community that they represent and serve, and ensuring a positive return on investment. Library 2.0 meets these needs, but it is up to you to make sure your board understands this advantage. You can appeal to their interests by explaining the benefits of Library 2.0. Library 2.0, for example, seeks to increase the library's user base. To the board, more satisfied library customers equal more satisfied citizens—taxpayers, students, or whomever the board represents. This should be an easy point to sell: the greater the success of the library, the greater the success of the board.

When explaining Library 2.0 to your library board, frame the discussion and presentation in business-like terminology. Ask them to consider the stakeholder returns and long-term profitability of successful change within the library. An upfront investment in Library 2.0 will equal long-term savings, either in the form of actual dollars saved in a more efficient, productive library or in the form of more users served per dollar spent. When first approaching the board, you will need solid ideas ready for approval; however, the governing board should also be included when formulating ideas for implementing Library 2.0. Participation on all levels is vital to the foundation of this model for library service. As staff and customers should be involved, so should your board. Invite them to participate in the formation of ideas for changes and new service creation. Although initially the board will need some solid ideas or examples to help its members buy in (they need to be able to see something), you will want them included on all fundamental levels of the process. This will allow the board to feel a sense of responsibility and pride over the positive changes enacted.

Library boards are often made up of members of the community, especially in public libraries. Consider selling your ideas by appealing to the interests of different board members and the groups they support. Who are your businessmen and businesswomen and entrepreneurs? They may understand the financial return on investment of your proposed changes. Do you have heavy supporters of specific community groups, such as home-schooling families, retirees, homemakers, social welfare organizations, the underprivileged, young adults and children, or homebound customers? If so, you can use this opportunity to promote the ways Library 2.0 will benefit these groups. Fundamental to library service is the desire to better serve library customers. Showing your board members ways you will better serve your community of users will demonstrate the benefits of positive changes within your organization.

Administration

Getting library administration to buy-in is similar to convincing the governing board. If you are the director or dean, you will likely have little problem asserting your authority; however, just because you are the person in charge does not automatically imply that your staff, including your administrators, agree with your vision of library service. When opinions differ, you will need to convince them of the virtues of your vision. Because Library 2.0 is a service model that promotes customer-driven services, and ultimately seeks to improve library service for your community of users, we would like to think that those who select librarianship as a profession will be ready to jump on board. Reality, however, is not so simple. There will be librarians, from those who have been in the profession for a few months to those who have been working in libraries for decades, who will fail to share your vision for Library 2.0 within your organization. Deal with this reluctance head on. Be assertive and honest about what you expect Library 2.0 to do for your library system and your customers. Explain your vision, but don't force it. Hopefully, most, if not all, of your administrators will get on board once they realize what Library 2.0 can do to revitalize your services. Once you have your administrative team on board, it will be easier to promote Library 2.0 to the rest of the staff.

If you are an administrator trying to get the rest of your administrative peers and your director on board, you will need to include a thorough explanation of the components and goals of Library 2.0 and what it can do for your organization's ability to better serve its customers before you can gain buy-in. Beyond this, you should provide as much research as possible when presenting the idea of Library 2.0, including what other libraries are doing, how you anticipate it working within your organization, and the means by which it can be accomplished. One primary concern may be the cost-effectiveness of Library 2.0. Certainly, some service offerings are more costly than others, so your budgetary constraints will need to be addressed in your proposal. Additionally, any change as significant as Library 2.0 involves significant staff time and effort; this will need to be addressed as well. If you can't do the research yourself to get an honest picture, can you convince your administrative team or director to create a team to conduct research into the feasibility of Library 2.0 and what it can do for your organization? This could be a first step in an organization that is reluctant to change or implement new ideas. Getting the research to back up what Library 2.0 will look like in your library, as well as an estimate of the costs and staff time involved, will take you much further when attempting to get your administrators and director on board.

Directors or administrators seeking administrative buy-in may need to tailor their pitch to different departments, such as materials, adult services, children's services, programming, and outreach. Consider the potential return on investment for each group, and tailor your approach accordingly. Departments and their staff will be more likely to buy in to change if you are open and honest, providing both the big picture as well as specific details. Let them know that their opinions will be heard. Explain the various components of Library 2.0 clearly, and assure administrators that their (and their staff's) active participation will be an integral part of the process.

Ask your department heads to think big and consider what could be accomplished by working together to enact positive change system-wide. How would they spend their budget, if it could be in any way they choose? Would they hire more staff, or would they create a new position to meet a need that is not currently being met? Maybe your IT department would like to hire a programmer to create tailor-made products specifically designed for your organization. Or, maybe your programs and outreach department will express a desire to hire a teen outreach librarian to pull in more young adults. How would they structure their own department differently, if given the option? What they ask for may very well be possible through Library 2.0.

Nonadministrative library staff members who are not in a position of official authority may have a more difficult time getting their administrative staff to learn about Library 2.0 and what it can do for their library. If you are fortunate enough to work for a library that already encourages and promotes staff feedback, use this opportunity to bring Library 2.0 to your administrators and peers. Numerous Library 2.0 blogs, Web sites, and articles can help you outline your case. If your administration has not yet heard of Library 2.0, or if you're not sure they have, bring it to them. Let them know what other libraries are doing and what may work for your organization.

Staff who lack easy or inviting opportunities to provide feedback or suggestions to administrators will obviously find it more difficult to get the word out about Library 2.0. It can be frustrating to be in a position where your input is not readily accepted. Getting the rest of the staff talking about and researching Library 2.0 can bolster your attempt to get the administrative team to listen. There is strength in numbers. If staff members are talking about Library 2.0, administrators will eventually take notice. You may also be pleasantly surprised and find that your director, administrators, and managers have already heard about Library 2.0 and what other libraries are doing to work toward this service model. Our main piece of advice for those staff members who are in organizations that are resistant to change is to continue talking and sharing ideas. Talk to whoever will listen.

Staff

While ultimately it may be most difficult to get staff to buy in to change, you may have an advantage in that you are at least attempting to sell it to them in the first place. Many respondents to the change survey stated that staff are often not included in conversations about change, and that their opinions are not consulted. Others reported that administrators rarely attempt to sell new ideas and changes to staff. In many organizations, staff tend to receive little or no warning before a big change is made—let alone information about the reasoning behind it. For that reason, the very fact that you are attempting to sell Library 2.0 to your staff shows your respect for their positions and the work that they do, and emphasizes your shared mission in your library or organization.

Staff will want to know how Library 2.0 will affect both the organization as a whole and them personally. Make sure you provide enough information so that staff will understand the positive aspects of the changes sought. Staff must feel like the administration and governing board will support them, and they will want to feel that their jobs and mission are well represented in any change. This is another reason to assure staff that they will be involved in the various levels of creation, implementation, and evaluation of new ideas.

Many respondents to the survey expressed the need for staff input at all levels when creating and implementing new services. One library science student wrote, "The staff or department that deal[s] with each particular issue should be heavily involved in creating and implementing those services." We also heard of the need for staff input to help achieve buy-in:

- "Staff should have the opportunity to be engaged. Management should actively seek input from staff in order to generate buy-in for new processes and change."

- "I think staff should play a major role in creating and implementing library services. You get better buy-in with involvement. You also get more, and better, ideas."

- "Staff needs to 'buy in' to the change for it to have a chance to work. To aid in this, staff should be a part of the service creation process so that they feel that the change is something they are a part of, not just something they are being told to do."

- "Staff are normally the ones that implement library services, so need to buy in to changes. Participation in developing services increases buy-in on implementation."

- "[Staff are] the ones working with the changes and selling them to the library patrons. You won't get staff buy-in unless they feel they have a hand in it."

The need for buy-in is particularly real for services that will require extensive customer training. Staff members who will be involved in introducing a new service to customers and responsible for training the customer on how to use it (e.g., RFID checkouts, downloadable media) must have input in the decision-making and implementation process. Keeping your staff informed and involved will make buy-in easier and make change a more positive experience for everyone involved. Staff involvement is discussed in more detail in Chapter 8.

Community

When discussing how to implement change and get everyone involved on board, we typically think about those who will need to approve, create, implement, or sustain the service or procedure being changed. It is also important, however, that we think about buy-in for those who will be using the services that have changed.

It is imperative that you get your library users involved in and accepting of change. Much as you keep your entire staff, administration, and board up-to-date with impending changes, you will also want to be sure that your customers are aware of what to look forward to. Without a doubt, whenever you make a significant change to a service or procedure, you will have customers who will feel put out. We have seen this several times over the years as libraries have evolved. For example, we still have customers who come into our libraries and wonder why we no longer have card catalogs. When libraries first migrated to computerized cataloging, they experienced resistance from library users who did not want what they saw as a perfectly acceptable method of information retrieval to change. Librarians worked with those customers who were at first upset or uncomfortable with this change by pointing out its benefits and teaching users how to use the new computerized catalog. Although today we still have customers (and librarians, for that matter) who reminisce about the old card catalog, we know that an online catalog better meets the needs of our users and staff.

Whenever you have a significant change approaching, such as a new ILS system or the implementation of RFID technology, it is imperative that you prepare not only your staff, but also your customers. Let them know in advance what to expect. Be proactive in getting the word out about the positives anticipated from the change. Will the new ILS system enable users to write reviews on their favorite books? Will the RFID system decrease customer wait times when checking out items? Let them know what they have to look forward to.

You'll also want to be clear on any changes that are likely to upset customers. For example, if while migrating to a new ILS system, the online catalog will be down for a week, be sure to let customers know in advance. The same is true when making decisions that will only affect a portion of your users. For example, if you are no longer ordering books on tape and instead only ordering books on CD due to a tight budget and decreasing interest in the tape format, consider ways to let those who still check out books on tape know about the change and what to expect. Make sure the reasons for the change are clearly understood by your staff, so that they can easily explain the reasoning to customers who question the change. Just as with your staff, administrators, and board, you are more likely to be successful with customers if you let them know what to expect when implementing changes.

Collaboration—Getting Everyone to Work Together

Getting everyone on board will make the transition to Library 2.0 smoother and more positive. Even when you are in the process of selling the concepts of Library 2.0 to the board, administration, staff, and your users, you will need to be clear on the need for collaboration among all involved. You will also want to think about customer input and use the feedback your users provide when making decisions about services and procedures. Consider creating a focus group of users from your community to provide direct feedback and assistance with the creation of new services and changes to current ones. One example is a Teen Advisory Board. Each branch of the Gwinnett County Public Library in Lawrenceville, Georgia, formed a Teen Advisory Board made up of willing and interested teens from the surrounding community to provide input and suggestions for ways to improve service to teens and get more young adults into the library. By expressing a genuine interest in what these teens had to say, each branch was able to gain valuable feedback that they used to increase their services to this age group.

It is also important for departments within your organization to work together. Consider all departments that will be involved in the implementation or maintenance of a service at the very beginning of the planning stage. If you expect the IT department to install public wireless in the building, make sure it is involved in the planning process. You would not let an accountant or adult services director choose which wireless router to purchase, since they would not know what would best meet the needs of your building and setup. You would want to ask someone who knows the technology, such as an IT department representative. A smooth transition requires having everyone who will be involved in implementing a new service represented in planning from the beginning. This concept of inclusion is discussed in detail in Chapter 4, and pointing out the benefits of this type of collaboration should assist you when seeking staff buy-in.

THE RELUCTANT PERSON OR DEPARTMENT

If you have not yet experienced the pleasure of working with the Reluctant Department or the Reluctant Person, you are quite lucky. This person or department usually has some key role in the success of a desired change, yet they want nothing to do with it. Dealing with someone who is not a team player is a topic for the management books, but it is important to briefly address this issue here, as many of you will face this challenge.

The reluctant person or department usually is resistant to any form of change, but is particularly disinterested in change that will affect they way they must do their job. The old saying, "you can't teach an old dog new tricks," though, doesn't apply here. There are plenty of new librarians and staff who detest change as much as some who have been in the field for years. Your organization must be proactive in forestalling any negative attitudes toward positive change for library users. We can provide you with some ideas for working with a reluctant person or department, but you will need to assess your own situation and determine what course of action will work best to resolve your particular issue.

One way to try and get reluctant staff members or departments on board is through promoting the positive aspects of Library 2.0. If you can get them motivated by highlighting the wonderful things that can be done to revitalize the library's services and better serve your customers, it is possible that they will understand the importance of getting on board. You can also try to persuade them through their peers. If their co-workers are excited about Library 2.0 and changes for your users, then hopefully these good attitudes will rub off on the reluctant persons. Letting the reluctant staff members or departments' fears and reasons for hesitating be heard may also help bring them around. Call them in for a chat and find out why they are reluctant; let them know that their concerns will be heard and considered. Just the knowledge that one has a voice tends to increase anyone's comfort level when facing change. If your reluctant persons or departments know that you are aware of their concerns, they may be more likely to get on board.

Finally, you can also help reluctant staff to feel like a genuine part of the process by actually involving them in the process. Think about making those who are hesitant a part of the teams that will enact change. Witnessing and participating in the process may lessen their concerns.

CONTINUING TO PROMOTE LIBRARY 2.0

After you have achieved buy-in from the majority of your staff, board, administrators, and customers, it will be incumbent on you to continue this success by maintaining interest and confidence in the benefits of Library 2.0. Once you have been successful in getting buy-in, you will now need to sustain that momentum by continuing to promote Library 2.0; we will discuss maintaining momentum further in Chapter 8.

One way to do so is through the use of teams, as outlined in Chapter 4. Vertical teams are particularly helpful in promoting Library 2.0, as these allow you to have people from all levels of your organization participate in the process. These same people will likely report back to their co-workers about their ability to provide valuable input for the organization. You will also want to continue to gather feedback from staff on all levels on how your current services are doing and about new services they believe your organization should consider. Knowing that your voice and the voices of your peers are being heard will help keep morale high.

Keeping your staff involved will contribute to their continued interest in the changes that will be occurring. Make sure that they are given the opportunity to participate in whatever ways they can, such as joining teams, assisting with the implementation of new services, training staff and customers, and providing feedback. When you involve them, they will not just feel like they are a part of the process, their contribution really will be valued. Most importantly, having your staff excited and actively working toward Library 2.0 keeps faith in the promise of better services for library users. Your staff will see positive, purposeful change in action.

8

Maintaining the Momentum

"Involving staff always results in better, more informed decisions, and it gives a sense of ownership to the staff."
—Patricia Uttaro

After getting everyone on board, you will need to think about ways to maintain the Library 2.0 momentum in your organization. You must continue to promote Library 2.0 to your staff, administration, board, and customers, even after obtaining initial buy-in. In this chapter, we will explain how to keep your staff interested and your services fresh through effective communication, planned staff involvement, and the quest for new ideas. Staff must keep an open mind for this process to work, and it is up to library administrators and managers to ensure that this happens. In order to keep the momentum, library employees must feel informed and that they are a part of the process.

COMMUNICATION

Effective communication is imperative for the smooth operation of any organization. Clear communication between departments and hierarchical levels creates a positive working environment for both staff and administration. An open, honest working atmosphere will make staff feel that they are a part of the process and allow them to take pride and feel a sense of ownership in the organization. This is true at all levels, from frontline staff, to shelvers, to managers, to administrators. Encourage active participation from all staff; everyone should feel as if they are a welcome part of the process. Free-flowing communication will help your organization maintain the momentum toward Library 2.0.

As a staff member, if you know what is expected of you, you are more likely to work confidently with the knowledge that you have clear objectives. Administrators and managers should keep their staff informed, not only about what changes to expect but also about why these changes will occur. When everyone involved knows what is expected of him or her, what to expect from others, and what to expect from the organization, staff will be happier and more productive.

Administration should be honest and forthcoming with information as is appropriate. If administration and library managers trust their staff, it will be much easier for the staff to return the sentiment. Let the lines of communication be fluid and work in both directions. Most of us have experienced working with a staff person who gives poor customer service and is not interested in providing the rest of us with assistance when needed. Don't be the person who gets annoyed when a staff person from a branch or another department calls or e-mails you with a question you think she should know the answer to. All this does is create a sour working environment; and, don't worry, the rest of the staff are well aware when you are typically crabby. If you supervise that person, make them stop. Everyone in your organization must provide excellent customer service, whether to your library users, vendors, or staff.

Library administrators who encourage and allow for open communication with their staff will see happier, more productive employees. Barriers that prevent the flow of information from top to bottom in both directions should be removed. Yes, situations may arise where it is unnecessary, or even counterproductive, for incomplete information around a given decision to be disseminated to lower-level staff. However, in most cases, open communication is crucial to a productive working environment. Staff who are aware of the reasoning behind a decision, as well as how that decision was made, are better able to support, implement, and explain this decision to customers. This is true for both significant and seemingly small changes.

Managers should not only give staff the reasons behind significant system-wide or administrative decisions, but should also provide information on seemingly minor decisions made at the local branch or department level. For example, one survey respondent shared the story of a public library branch manager who decided to move newly purchased fiction from a small, inadequate shelving unit located near the front lobby to a larger shelving unit in a well-lit area adjacent to the Adult Fiction section—yet much farther from the front door. Although the change was made for good reasons, staff members were not informed. Shortly after the relocation, customers who frequently browsed the new books asked frontline staff about the reasons for the change. Since frontline staff members were aware that the books had been moved but not of the reasoning behind the shift, customers received varied answers to their questions, ranging from, "It wasn't being used," to "We needed more room for all the books," to "I don't know." When staff are inadequately informed and unable to explain to customers the reasoning behind a change, this creates a negative situation for both staff and customers. The more vigilant customers, who asked several staff members, came away with several different answers and the thought that: "I guess the response as to why something was done depends on who you ask," or, "No one here knows what's going on."

In this example, the branch manager moved the new book section for positive reasons, hoping that it would improve customer experience in the library. However, because the frontline staff was not given a reason for the change, they were not able to provide customers with a clear, consistent explanation for the move. All of this could have been avoided if staff had been given a simple explanation, such as, "While many of our customers enjoy convenient access to new fiction by the lobby, by relocating it closer to the Adult Fiction section, we were able to provide a larger shelf space and more comfortable, well-lit conditions in which to browse." If staff had been given this information, it could have been relayed to customers, possibly relieving some anxiety over the move. Even further, the branch manager could have explained that the decision stemmed from several customer suggestions that the library find a better place for the new books.

Not only should library managers and staff communicate openly, but it is also imperative that the library board and director effectively communicate with each other. In most cases, the director brings ideas for change to the board for final consideration, which have already been considered, evaluated, and planned by qualified library staff. You will want to make sure the board is informed of the plans and processes involved in creating, implementing, and reviewing ideas and services. The board, though, should not interfere with this process; rather, it should be aware of and informed about it.

It is important that the library board have faith that the library professionals hired will use their informed professional opinions to create services that will best meet the needs of the community. It can be difficult when a library board attempts to micromanage the organization, particularly if board members lack a library science education or professional library experience—which is almost always the case. Remember, the board and library staff do have the same goal of improving library service. It is incumbent on library staff to use their professional knowledge in working with the board to reach that goal. Acknowledge that board members are trying to be active in their role as representatives of the community and as a governing body over the organization, and do your best to prevent any conflict from stifling growth and impeding service to your users. A board is completely justified in wanting to know how and why certain processes are carried out. By keeping the board informed, you will save a lot of headaches and make board members feel that they are a part of the process (because, really, they *are* a part of the process).

STAFF AND CUSTOMER INVOLVEMENT

Tap into one of your library's most valuable resources—your staff! As mentioned in the previous section, library administrators must encourage and allow for open communication with their staff; staff on all levels must be involved in the process of creating, implementing, and evaluating ideas and services at all times. It is the administration's responsibility to ensure that staff members are able to remain involved. Making an effort to involve staff will only enrich your service offerings.

Librarian Eric L. Frierson explains, "Librarians and other staff members, as the main interface for users of the library, have a significant role in the brainstorming, creation, design, and evaluation of library services. In any library system, I'm sure those who have chosen this profession are creative and public service-oriented individuals who can collaborate and develop amazing new services for library users." Library staff and administrators who we surveyed agree; staff are well positioned to provide input. That input can be a valuable asset when creating and evaluating library services. Who better to let administrators know what customers want than those who interact with customers the most? Survey respondents said:

- "I think the staff should definitely play a part in coming up with ideas, perhaps in the form of focus groups. The staff are the ones who have to carry out the changes with the public and are the only ones to have a realistic viewpoint on what the patrons need and want."

- "Staff should be involved—they can have insights into how things are actually functioning in implementation, what practical things need to be taken into consideration. Plus programs 'imposed from on high' tend to die a painful death if the staff doesn't feel connected to them."

- "I think feedback from the staff, especially those who work the desks (circ, reference, etc.), should have a major role. They have the most contact with the users of the library."

- "I think staff should be given a great deal of leeway and encouragement to create and implement services—either new ones or current ones in a new way—provided that they communicate with everyone who needs to know. Library staff need support to be entrepreneurial and library administration should foster attempts to try new approaches."

- "Staff are a critical part of creating services because they are by necessity part of the implementation."

- "Staff who work with users should identify needs and study proposed solutions for meeting those needs. Staff should work on the implementation, promotion, and teaching of all services."

- "I think that staff are in an optimum position to know what is needed in terms of user requirements and service enhancements—even if they don't necessarily have the tech knowledge to develop the solutions, they are the ones who know how it will be used and whether it will be of use to users."

- "From an IT standpoint, staff should be very involved and allowed to experiment with new technologies (even if that's just a free Web site like del.icio.us, or IM). Once they get excited about it, they'll be eager to use the technology and to promote it to the patrons."

As one librarian mentioned: "The staff are key to making things happen, but they need the time and opportunity to explore and learn new services to implement them correctly." Certainly, we must listen to what staff have to offer, and extend the opportunity to actively participate in the research, implementation, and evaluation of services. This two-way river of communication between administrators and staff should be open at all times, but is especially important when evaluating specific services or duties. Administrators should communicate with the very staff members who are most intimate with these processes. They can be your best resource in understanding what is working, what's not, and what improvements could be made.

For example, when evaluating an ILL service, we should not only collect the experiences and opinions of the staff who process ILL requests; we must also speak with those who deal directly with the customers requesting ILLs. The librarians and library support staff who broker ILL requests are likely to provide valuable insight into what customers are seeking in an ILL service and why they are using it. (Of course, in this example, as throughout Library 2.0, we should also consider the opinions and needs of the customers who actually request ILLs.)

Not only should you seek feedback from the staff involved, you should also seriously consider what they have to say when making decisions. This sounds obvious, but how often have we polled staff or customers, only to make a decision based on incomplete or even false data? It is imperative that we not view gathered data in a way that only tells us what we want to hear.

One way to keep staff involved is through participation on organizational teams or committees. Vertical teams are an important part of staff involvement. From the three teams discussed in Chapter 4 (investigative team, planning team, and review team) to any other teams your library may have, staff from different levels should be involved. There also should be easy ways for staff to volunteer to join teams, such as through a system-wide call for new members. Good judgment must be used when determining how team members will be selected, in order to maintain a good balance of members. Each team should have members with direct knowledge about the team's charge or goal, such as having an IT staff member on a planning team for creating an RFID upgrade. Each team should also have members from various levels of the organization. In this RFID example, you would want your team to have at least one frontline staff member, as the frontline staff will assist customers with this new technology. You would also want to have staff from various departments and administration for balance. On any team, consider having a mix of members, such as both new and seasoned staff, tech-savvy staff, customer-service oriented staff, and both introverts and extroverts. Keeping staff from various areas and backgrounds within the organization involved will keep their morale up and help your organization maintain momentum toward Library 2.0 and better serving your library customers.

Encourage staff feedback by creating ways for staff to submit suggestions for services or procedures. It is imperative that staff are given the freedom to be candid, yet professional, when sharing ideas and providing feedback. An easy and unintimidating mechanism for staff suggestions can boost morale and provide an excellent source for new ideas. In order for this to be successful, staff members need to be sure that their ideas and suggestions will be heard and taken seriously. Similarly, your organization should also have a way for frontline staff to communicate customer ideas and suggestions to their supervisors and library administrators. Your frontline staff who deal directly with your users on a daily basis are an excellent resource. They know best what your organization's customers want and need. They must be made to feel comfortable sharing the suggestions of customers, or even their own observations of what customers are asking for or need. These staff members can tell you what is being requested that you don't offer or have. They can tell you what types of questions they are getting and what types of resources they are most often providing.

As discussed in Chapter 6, an internal blog is one example of a tool that staff can use to provide input. An open blog that calls for ideas could be used by all staff to comment and make suggestions. This would be an easy way for frontline staff to share what they know from their experiences and for the rest of the staff to have an opportunity to openly discuss ideas and suggestions. This type of blog could either be part of a general system-wide blog, or a special "Idea Blog" that is created solely for this purpose. If your organization decides to create a team system like that in the Three Branches of Change example from Chapter 4, your investigative team could use the information from this blog to supplement its own research when coming up with ideas to investigate. Once again, having your staff involved in the process of change and Library 2.0 will keep the momentum going. In addition to the Idea Blog, your organization should also consider internal blogs on the branch or departmental level, which can be a great resource for staff to communicate ideas.

One alternative to blogs is a simple online form that staff can use to submit suggestions directly to supervisors, administrators, or a team designated to handle staff suggestions, such as the investigative team. The downside of this method is that you won't have the benefit of feedback from the rest of the staff that you get from multiple comments on a blog. Whichever avenue your organization uses to collect staff input, though, all suggestions must be taken seriously. Either a team or an administrator must be responsible for ensuring these ideas are heard.

You will also need to consider the best way for customers to submit ideas and suggestions. An old-fashioned suggestion box or online form could work fine, as long as the input is taken seriously. If your library does not offer word-processing software, for instance, but you continually get suggestions from customers requesting this service, you should not just ignore your users. Even if a decision was made at some point that your library would not offer word processing, this does not automatically mean that your library must never offer this service. Libraries don't need to automatically change a service because one or two people yell loudly. However, we must be willing to investigate the feasibility of customer suggestions, and always be willing to revisit previous decisions. Take your users seriously, and consider the suggestions that they make.

If you are daring, you could also create a public blog for your customers to use to comment on the library and its services. The downside to this is that you expose yourself both to positive comments and to harsh criticism. This is a decision that your organization will probably want to consider carefully. Staff can monitor comments, removing or disallowing those that are profane or inflammatory, but it is inadvisable to prevent any critical discussion of the library, its services, or its staff.

When developing methods for staff and customers to communicate their ideas, your most important consideration is to remember that, no matter what, staff and customers must always feel that their voices are heard. Clear channels of communication that keep ideas or suggestions from getting lost will boost confidence and help you maintain the momentum toward Library 2.0.

How to Look for New Ideas

Looking for new ideas for services can be challenging, yet very rewarding for library staff. Your organization will keep the Library 2.0 momentum going by encouraging your staff and customers to be a part of the process on a continual basis. New ideas should not only be the province of one or two people; make sure all staff and customers are given an opportunity to participate in the brainstorming process.

When trying to come up with new ideas, your organization should look both at itself and at other organizations and industries. When looking inward, consider what methods you have in place to find out what your customers want and need. Whether you use surveys, comment cards, or online forms for feedback, understand: Whom better to tell you what your customers want, than your customers themselves? Also, think about older services that either failed, or were scrapped before they could be implemented. Why did a particular service fail? Why did your organization decide not to implement a certain service? In particular, services that are frequently requested by customers or staff should be reconsidered on a regular basis to ascertain whether the reasons behind the decision not to provide these services are still valid.

You will also want to think about what other libraries are doing to meet customer needs. By looking beyond the collective knowledge of your staff and customers, you can gain a diverse and well-rounded perspective of library service. Consider sending staff around to local libraries to chat with their staff. You can bring back great ideas and also see what worked and did not work for a particular organization. Do not be afraid to borrow ideas from other libraries. Many libraries and librarians are now blogging about their experiences with new and different services and are eager to share their successful ideas.

The Emerging Technologies Team

Looking outside your library, and outside librarianship in general, to the tools being used by others is one of the best ways to find and evaluate new technologies. The Gwinnett County [GA] Public Library has been utilizing an Emerging Technologies Team since it was first started several years ago by former technology services director Sue Calbreath and former executive director Jo Ann Pinder.

The charge of the team is to examine both new technologies and technologies that may be new to the library world but are in use in other organizations. Many of the technology products the team examines are either new to the market or are in early beta stages. Some products are only being used by a handful of institutions. There are several prerequisites for effectively evaluating these tools, including an open mind, an ability to think beyond the library's current boundaries and structure, and an understanding of how technologies will ultimately work and play together.

When choosing members to serve on this team, it is important to pick staff members who bring with them some expertise, or a strong interest in an area of technology that the team leader and other team members may be lacking. If your own area of interest lies, say, in networking, then also choose some team members who appreciate and understand Web services, electronic gaming, or multimedia creation. Also, try to choose several frontline staff. Their practical understanding of day-to-day library operations and real-life customer service issues will help the entire team stay focused. It may also be beneficial to include one or two of your IT personnel. IT team members bring with them two very important attributes: a wealth of understanding regarding technology in general, and a firm knowledge of the library's current technology. This knowledge allows them to picture and explain how the products being evaluated may eventually fit into the library's technology infrastructure.

Having IT staff members on the team does something else, too—it puts the IT department on notice that things *do* change, and that the library's technology will always need to progress. Having IT on board during this part of the process ensures early buy-in and a much easier job selling the idea when it comes to the budget; it eliminates the sometimes difficult job of selling the new product or service to the IT department. When they are a part of the process from the earliest stages, IT staff members are integral players and have an interest in seeing the initiative succeed.

In 2006, Gwinnett County Public Library's Emerging Technologies Team began holding informal meetings over lunch and inviting various library staff and library users to sit down, join in, and talk about some of the technology issues they face. This sharing of ideas and collaborative problem solving has directly resulted in several new technologies being integrated into the library system. This type of interaction also allows team members to hear from individuals whom they might otherwise rarely get to interact with. Inviting top-level administrative staff to such meetings lets the educational process flow in both directions. Team members get a realistic and honest assessment of technology needs from the administration, and the administration gets to hear about some of the more exciting technology possibilities on the horizon.

It is also worth thinking about inviting outside officials and library board members to regular team meetings. These prominent community leaders often have friends and acquaintances who use new technologies in unique ways, and who also have the ability to make things happen. Want to try and sell a new self-check system to the board and your community? What better way to work toward a successful approval process than to have a board member or local leader champion your cause?

The value of such a team is great and bound only by the creativity and energy of its leader. By enlisting frontline staff and administrators, library users, and community leaders, your emerging technologies team will be well positioned to find, evaluate, and implement tools that will serve your library well.

Old-fashioned networking is another great way to discover what other libraries are doing to meet customer needs. When you attend any conference, make sure you float around and meet people from other libraries. Even libraries that seem the exact opposite of your own can provide valuable insight into new services your customers may enjoy. Don't be afraid to ask a fellow librarian how his library performs a particular task, collects customer or staff feedback, or implements new ideas. Organizations love to toot their own horns, so people you meet at conferences will be happy to share their ideas and what has worked for their libraries. Don't forget to reciprocate by sharing your own success stories.

There are other options, if your organization is not often able to send staff to conferences. Consider, for instance, bringing a speaker in to address your staff. Increasingly, you can also find Web-based conferences and continuing education opportunities, many of which are free. You can also research what other libraries are doing by reading the library literature. Professional journals and library magazines constantly publish "how we did it here" stories. You can use this information to get new ideas and to learn from other organizations' mistakes and successes.

Don't be afraid to look outside the library world. Libraries have a lot to learn from companies in other industries that successfully meet their consumers' needs while maintaining a satisfied workforce. Think big, and think globally. Look at companies or industries that seem extremely different from libraries, and then try to find a connection. See what services they offer that may provide insight into your own customers' changing needs.

KEEPING AN OPEN MIND

Your library will not become a Library 2.0 organization overnight; it will require hard work and dedication from all levels of staff. Once you have created a plan for reaching your Library 2.0 goals and have obtained buy-in from your board, administrators, and staff, you will need to keep the momentum going. Encourage effective, open communication among staff and ensure that this communication is fluid among all levels in the organization. Keep the lines open and let the information flow in both directions. Your staff, administration, and governing board must be involved in the input and decision-making process for new ideas and services. Look for new ideas both within your organization and through researching other libraries and businesses.

If you take anything away from this chapter, let it be that you must keep an open mind to new ideas in order to keep staff motivated and the Library 2.0 momentum going. Sure, there will be services that will work for one library that might not be successful at your organization or a good fit with your community. Still, if staff members on all levels keep their minds open and think creatively, your organization will find itself swimming in great ideas for improving library service.

9

Final Considerations

"What we do is vital, and only by addressing the changes in our society are we going to stay that way."
—Sandra Stewart

Library 2.0 is about change. It's about making change in your organization easy and routine. It's about updating the services we offer and creating new services that will reach out to community members who do not yet make use of our great facilities and offerings. Library 2.0 seeks to bring staff on board and include them in our decision-making processes. Frontline staff know our customers better than anyone else, and we need to harness that knowledge in our effort to reach out to the community and improve our services.

Library 2.0 is also about politics. It's about funding, and community support, and building a base of supporters who will vote for library-friendly politicians and library-sponsored initiatives. The technologies and services that we have discussed, and more importantly, the structures designed to facilitate change, are all designed to make our current users more satisfied and to bring in new users. Like any business hoping to expand its customer base, libraries need to look outward with the ultimate goal of serving more people, and serving them better.

We hear politicians and prognosticators say that the library is being supplanted by the Internet (aka Google), and we respond with the ill-contrived argument that people will somehow always need us because

Google doesn't work. This simply is not true. Google may not give everyone the best answer, but it is the user who determines usefulness, not us. If Google users think they are getting good answers, then they will stick with Google.

We worry about what will happen tomorrow because we are not in charge of today. But librarians do not have crystal balls that allow us to see into the future. We cannot be sure that tomorrow there will not be another service that will take more users from us. No library, or library board, should be looking into the proverbial crystal ball for the future of the library. The library and its leadership need to be shaping that future today by crafting services that people want now.

This is perhaps easier said than done, but the power is in each library's hands to shape itself and to grow to meet its users' needs. The tools to do just that are being discussed here in this book, and at conferences, on blogs, and throughout the library world. We shape our own future, but we cannot do that if we sit back and simply watch. The library that is flexible, listens to its community, and changes to meet changing demand and demographics will be the library that succeeds, prospers, and pushes its mission out to the most citizens.

A LIBRARY 2.0 LIBRARY

It is hard to describe what a Library 2.0 library would look like, as this is not a one-size-fits-all model. We can, though, attempt a description of what one library might look like when it applies the Library 2.0 concepts: constant and purposeful change and user participation, with the goal of better serving current users and reaching potential users:

> A medium-sized public library with a steady, yet stagnant, budget and open-minded administration and board seeks to apply the Library 2.0 model to its organizational structure. The community that the library serves is a culturally and economically diverse population that is growing steadily. Much of the population is computer literate; however, there is still

a large number of citizens who do not own a computer or have any means of Internet access other than through the library. The library has tried to keep up with emerging technologies over the years, and has recently added RFID self-checkout machines and downloadable books. Staffing is tight, so outreach efforts have been limited over the past couple of years.

The library has created a written plan for evaluating all library services and procedures over time. While reviewing all services takes time, with the plan in place, library staff know that in the near future (and on a regular schedule) these evaluations will occur. To begin with, the library has created a master list of library services, which is updated regularly to reflect new or discontinued service offerings. Each of these services is assigned a regular review date, which depends on the service itself. The library's written plan calls for, in part, two permanent teams to help the organization achieve Library 2.0 goals. Both teams are vertical by design, meaning that they include staff from all levels, from administrators to managers to frontline staff. One team, called the investigation team (I-Team), processes staff and customer ideas, as well as reviews system statistics to determine what services are being used and which ones might need reevaluating. The primary charge of this team is to consider the feasibility of these suggested changes and make official recommendations as to which services should be added or reviewed for termination. Whenever the I-Team makes a recommendation for the addition of a new service, a new team, called the planning team (P-Team), is created. This team includes staff from various departments, particularly staff from those departments that have a role in the implementation, maintenance, or marketing of the service. This team creates both an implementation plan and a review plan for the service. The second permanent team, called the

review team (R-Team), handles the evaluation of all services and procedures, including those called for review by
the I-Team. The R-Team's primary charge is to thoroughly
evaluate each service to determine whether it is meeting
stated goals and is still meeting customer needs as it currently operates. If necessary, this team will suggest changes
to update or improve the service or procedure.

Woven throughout all of this is the use of staff and customer input. Each library branch has a suggestion station,
which includes simple forms on which customers and staff
can provide feedback. Suggestions can also be submitted
electronically through the library's Web site. Each form that
is submitted, either in person or electronically, is reviewed
by the I-Team. This method of evaluation through consistent research and consideration of customer and staff feedback allows the library to have constant change imbedded
within the organizational structure.

Customers are also given a participatory role in the services
the library offers, in ways beyond just feedback and suggestions. Customer-generated content, including material
reviews, tags, and suggested reading lists, much like those on
Amazon, is created right in the catalog for all library users to
see. Library customers are invited to participate in a library-
created blog, where they can offer feedback and suggestions
regarding library services. Customers also are invited to participate in programming events. When a popular author came
to visit recently, the event was podcast through the library's
Web site, and viewers were able to call in, e-mail, IM, or text
message questions from their cell phones that the author could
then answer. Of course, this was in addition to all of the questions and input that audience members at the actual event were
able to provide. The library also invites members of the community to call together book discussions, language immersion

classes, knitting groups, and other community meeting events, using whatever space is available in the library.

The library also attempts to reach those users who are not currently using its services. It conducted a community feedback survey of those who claim they do not use the library. An overwhelming number of responses indicated that the library did not have the titles that these potential customers would want. Many customers were not aware of the interlibrary loan service. While the library wanted to satisfy these customers, doing so using the traditional interlibrary loan service would be costly. After reviewing the high costs of interlibrary loan, the library instituted a purchase-on-demand service as a means for filling most interlibrary loan requests, and launched a marketing campaign on its Web site, in the branches, and in the local newspaper. While interlibrary loan is still utilized for some expensive or out-of-scope items, the majority of interlibrary loan requests are filled by purchasing inexpensive, used items through online retailers such as Amazon. If it is determined that there is likely to be a demand beyond the single customer request, the item is added to the library's collection. If not, the item is sold through the library's book sale. This method has proven itself to be an extremely cost-effective way of reaching part of the Long Tail of users who were not before using the library.

It is important to remember that changing your organizational structure cannot happen overnight. You also need staff, administrators, and possibly members of the governing board to buy into organizational changes. Although this can be difficult to deal with, it can be done. It may take months to years for your organization to run smoothly under the Library 2.0 model. One thing to consider is, are you really running smoothly now? Is it not worth a try to make your library more appealing and useful for your users?

Appendix A: Survey

Many of the stories, comments, and quotes in this book come from a survey the authors conducted about change and libraries. The survey Libraries, Librarians, and Change was posted online using SurveyMonkey in April 2006. The purpose of the survey was to receive firsthand impressions, experiences, and opinions regarding change and libraries. The survey had the following preface:

Thank you for taking the time to answer this short survey about libraries, librarians, and change. We are interested in knowing how change affects services, procedures, and other operations within your library.

By participating, you are giving your permission to be quoted in a forthcoming book from Information Today, as well as in supporting materials on the topic (e.g., articles, promotional materials, blogs, presentations). Please be sure to indicate whether you would like to remain anonymous. If you wish to remain anonymous, identifying details about you and your institution will be deleted from quoted answers. If you do not wish to answer a particular question, please leave it blank.

SURVEY QUESTIONS

1. Name
2. E-mail address
3. If your answers are quoted, do you wish to remain anonymous? Yes / No
4. Which best describes your library? Public / Academic / School / Special / Other (please specify)
5. Which best describes your current job? Administration / Management / Librarian / Support Staff / Other (please specify)
6. Position / Title
7. Organization
8. City
9. State
10. ZIP
11. Do you have an MLS/MSLIS? Yes / No / I'm a library science student
12. If yes, what year and where did you receive your degree?
13. What year did you begin working in libraries?
14. Do you feel that, overall, your library changes … Too much / Just the right amount / Not enough / Other (please specify)
15. What stimulates change in your library? Check all that apply. Administrative decisions / Committees or teams / User feedback, surveys, or focus groups / Staff feedback, surveys, or focus groups / Other (please specify)
16. How frequently are staff involved in providing input or making decisions that affect services, procedures, and other operations within your library? Always / Sometimes / Rarely / Never
17. Please elaborate if desired.
18. What role do you think staff should play in creating and implementing library services?

19. In your organization, what can staff do to get a library service, procedure, or policy changed?

20. Does your library have regularly scheduled evaluations of services, procedures, and policies? Yes / No / Somewhere in between (please elaborate)

21. Do you think that your library consistently offers the services that library users want? Yes / No / Sometimes

22. Please elaborate if desired.

23. What do you think libraries need to do to keep up with the changing needs of library users?

24. What do you think libraries can do to reach new users?

25. We welcome any additional comments about libraries, librarians, and change.

RESPONSE

A total of 365 people completed the survey. Respondents included librarians, support staff, managers, administrators, library science students, and library service vendors. Although the majority of respondents were from either public or academic libraries, several school and special librarians also completed the survey. An overwhelming 74.5 percent of respondents reported having a MLS/MSLIS, and 8.8 percent were enrolled in a library science program. A wide range of experience was represented; several respondents reported first working in libraries as early as 1964, while many respondents entered the field as recently as 2005.

The majority of the respondents indicated an awareness of the need for change within their organizations. Many responses described the need for libraries to listen to their users and respond accordingly. The majority of respondents also felt that, in order for libraries to keep up with the changing needs of users, library staff must continually educate themselves. Overall, the survey demonstrated that librarians do collectively realize that libraries and their staff must be prepared to change. Without change, libraries risk losing their relevance.

Following are charts and select quotes from the survey. Additional survey quotes and statistics are available on the book's companion Web site (www.librarychange.com).

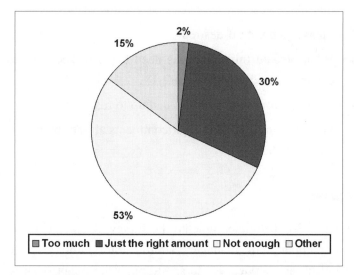

Survey Question: Do you feel that, overall, your library changes …

What stimulates change in your library?

- "Mostly conversations among staff … based on our observations [and] interactions with patrons."

- "Usually it's a result of outside forces [and] necessity [and] to a lesser extent, suggestions from administration or other staff."

- "Parents supply our budget and may choose to fund—or not fund—projects which we propose."

- "When forced to. For example, Wal-Mart drops VHS, resulting in fewer VHS being produced, which means library can't get the VHS it would normally buy, thus forcing a change to DVD."

- "[B]ad publicity (i.e., reacting to negative news comparing the library with other local libraries implementing change)."

- "Information from conferences and meetings, whether attended in person, or reading conference blogs."

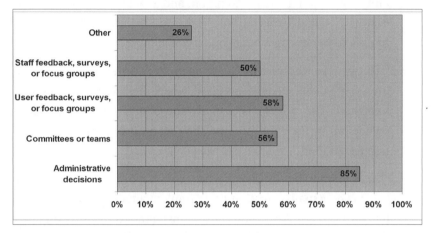

Survey Question: What stimulates change in your library? Check all that apply.

What role do you think staff should play in creating and implementing library services?

- "Staff should have an active role; they are often the ones out there on the frontlines and have to be the ones to implement them. At the same time, staff can't always have a say in every single thing that affects their job. Libraries can be giant bureaucracies as it is; at some point a decision needs to be made. I also think staff are a valuable resource for creating new services. It's important that there be a culture where staff are encouraged to make suggestions, and those suggestions are taken seriously. Nothing is more frustrating than hearing 'we want to hear your ideas,' only to never see any new ideas implemented."

- "I think they should be instrumental in helping with changes to services and functions. They are on the front lines working with people all the time, so they have a good sense of what they need and want."

- "I think staff should always have input. If staff can provide and supply a new concept, it should be considered. Not every idea flies, but they should be addressed."

- "Staff should play a HUGE role, but they need to take responsibility for learning what's going on, and acquaint themselves with user needs and expectations, rather than basing decisions on long-held beliefs or models of service that may be outdated."

- "The people who provide a service or perform a task should be involved in the 'change process' when their service or task is impacted. The trouble is, usually these staff have no sense of ownership of their job because they've been browbeaten or bullied for so long."

- "Staff should be involved—they can have insights into how things are actually functioning in implementation, what practical things need to be taken into consideration. Plus programs 'imposed from on high' tend to die a painful death if the staff doesn't feel connected to them."

- "That's very hard to answer since every library is so different. Staff should contribute according to their abilities and expertise. [E]veryone should be able to make suggestions outside of his or her specialty."

In your organization, what can staff do to get a library service, procedure, or policy changed?

- "I've found suggesting the change to the relevant supervisor or manager to be most effective, so long as that supervisor or manager is open to the idea of doing things differently [or] better."

- "Sometimes simply making a suggestion will do it; sometimes months of gentle, repeated suggesting (read 'hectoring' or 'nagging') is necessary."

- "The only path is to approach the director."

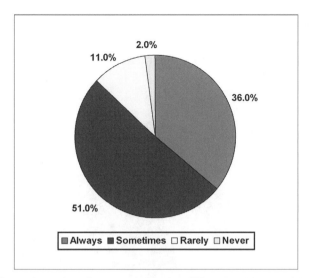

Survey Question: How frequently are staff involved in providing input or making decisions that affect services, procedures, and other operations within your library?

- "Staff are encouraged to first speak to their direct supervisors (or the person in charge of the area they'd like to see changed). Our administrative team of directors is all open to hearing suggestions also, if someone wants to go that route. It also helps an idea get a listen if you have constructive suggestions for changes, not just complaints about something needing to be changed."

- "I would have to speak to my supervisor, other persons with seniority, and then try to get our library 'opinion leaders' (who aren't always savvy) on board with the concept."

- "Pretty much just bring it up. The managers will kick it around, we might open it up to staff feedback, discuss it in a staff meeting, and then make it happen."

- "Talking to your supervisor is the best way to advocate for change. Participating in working groups is another established route. There's also a suggestion box for anonymous feedback."

- "The most effective method is to work through one of our many committees, task forces, or project teams. A staff member can also work directly with a supervisor to initiate change."

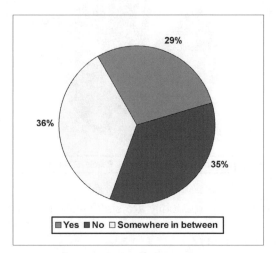

Survey Question: Does your library have regularly scheduled evaluations of services, procedures, and policies?

What do you think libraries need to do to keep up with the changing needs of library users?

- "Provide the staff with a voice to promote needed changes and be able to have the opportunity to explain to those in charge why these changes are needed and who they're for—the patrons! We're the ones who work with the library users on a daily basis, and we're the ones who have the best 'feel' for what their needs are."

- "Try to keep an eye on not only what services people are using, and what services people are asking for, but also on what services people are going elsewhere to get. For example: Are people spending more time at the bookstore than the library? What does the bookstore have that the library doesn't? (Hours? Location? Comfortable seating? etc.)"

- "Consistently solicit and LISTEN to feedback."

- "Understand our customers and their changing needs. Talking to our users, reading about how the coming generations are changing their information seeking behaviors and use of technology."

- "We should be ready and willing to see the change, create the change, and be the change."

- "Keep a close eye on demographics, what and how successful businesses in the area are marketing, and pay attention to, even solicit, frontline staff opinions and ideas."

- "Outreach, especially to people who don't use the library. Look beyond books to fill our library."

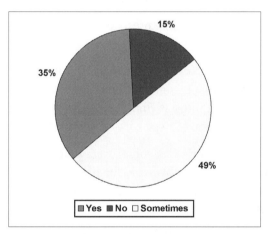

Survey Question: Do you think that your library consistently offers the services that library users want?

What do you think libraries can do to reach new users?

- "Try new outreach methods. Do more on the Web. Get Flickr accounts, use blogs, try MySpace. Do anything that might work and hasn't been tried before or recently."

- "Look at the needs and interests of some of the people who aren't showing up (e.g., the skateboarders in the parking lot). Find a way to meet some of those needs and interests (skateboarding books, Web links, music popular with the local skateboarding subculture, maybe a speaker). And, let the potential users know about what's available. As a middle school library, we usually use the morning announcements, posters, or tracking down a kid from the group and showing the kid what we've got."

- "In our situation, we can make a personal effort to make a connection. We can also use their peers and faculty to reach out to them about the value of the library in their education."

- "Marketing, advertising. Let underserved groups know how the library can be useful. Tell patrons to tell their friends that their research questions were answered at the library."

- "Create a more engaging presence that offers something users see as unique and innovative."

- "Podcasts, RSS, roadshows, e-mail. Tailor service to the different stakeholder groups—international researchers in science don't want the same things as first-year undergraduates in English, but we tend to offer a one-size-fits-all service."

- "I think technology has some ways that might reach new users who would traditionally avoid the library. We need to reach out to them in a space where they feel comfortable rather than expect them to be dazzled by our brilliance and come into our physical building. Things like podcasts, blogs, Flickr, tags might be ways we could reach some new users."

- "Be personable, approachable, and useful."

- "Multiple things: Reach out with new technologies; have staff who reflect the population served; offer services in more languages than just English and Spanish; be more visible in the community."

Appendix B:
Referenced Web Sites

The following is a list of Web sites mentioned in the book (in the order in which they appear). We will maintain this list of sites on the book's Web page (www.librarychange.com) to reflect updated or changed links.

INTRODUCTION

LibraryCrunch, www.librarycrunch.com
SurveyMonkey, www.surveymonkey.com

CHAPTER 1: BRAND LIBRARY 2.0

OCLC's *Perceptions of Libraries and Information Resources*, www.oclc.org/reports/2005perceptions.htm

CHAPTER 2: THE ESSENTIAL INGREDIENTS

My Yahoo!, my.yahoo.com
Google News, news.google.com
Flickr, www.flickr.com
Amazon, www.amazon.com
Netflix, www.netflix.com

CHAPTER 3: FINDING THE ROAD TO LIBRARY 2.0

AquaBrowser Library, www.medialab.nl

Ellsworth Public Library, www.ellsworth.lib.me.us

Dallas Public Library, www.dallaslibrary.org

Madeleine Clark Wallace Library, Wheaton College, www.wheaton
ma.edu/library

North Harris College Library, nhclibrary.nhmccd.edu

Bloomfield Public Library, www.bplnj.org

Las Vegas-Clark County Library District, www.lvccld.org

Georgia Tech Library and Information Center, www.library.gatech.edu

WebTrends, www.webtrends.com

clickdensity, www.clickdensity.com

CHAPTER 5: PARTICIPATORY SERVICE AND THE LONG TAIL

Amazon, www.amazon.com

FactCheck.org, www.factcheck.org

Wikipedia, www.wikipedia.org

Waterboro Public Library Blog, www.waterborolibrary.org/blog.htm

Darien Library Director's Blog, www.darienlibrary.org/directorsblog

eBay, www.ebay.com

Netflix, www.netflix.com

Niagara University Library Netflix ILL Service, www.niagara.edu/
library/illdvds.html

Ann Arbor District Library, www.aadl.org

Gwinnett County Public Library, www.gwinnettpl.org

Stephen's Lighthouse, stephenslighthouse.sirsi.com

Tacoma Public Library, www.tacomapubliclibrary.org

Darien Library, www.darienlibrary.org

CHAPTER 6: INCORPORATING TECHNOLOGY

Google Maps, maps.google.com

Zoho, www.zoho.com

Google Docs, docs.google.com

37 Signals, www.37signals.com

Skype, www.skype.com

TechCrunch, www.techcrunch.com

Blogger, www.blogger.com

WordPress, www.wordpress.org

Moveable Type, www.sixapart.com/movabletype

LiveJournal, www.livejournal.com

WordPress.com, www.wordpress.com

TypePad, www.typepad.com

Xanga, www.xanga.com

Drupal, www.drupal.org

Ann Arbor District Library, www.aadl.org

Bloglines, www.bloglines.com

Netvibes, www.netvibes.com

Wikia, www.wikia.com/wiki/Wikia

JotSpot, www.jotspot.com

PBwiki, www.pbwiki.com

SeedWiki, www.seedwiki.com

Wikispaces, www.wikispaces.com

MediaWiki, www.mediawiki.org

TWiki, www.twiki.org

XWiki, www.xwiki.org

Saint Joseph County Public Library's Subject Guides, www.libraryfor
life.org/subjectguides/index.php/Main_Page

Zoho Chat, zohochat.com

Campfire, www.campfirenow.com

AIM, www.aim.com

Yahoo! Messenger, messenger.yahoo.com

Windows Live Messenger, messenger.msn.com

Google Talk, www.google.com/talk

Trillian (for PC), www.ceruleanstudios.com

Fire (for Mac), fire.sourceforge.net

Gaim, gaim.sourceforge.net

meebo, www.meebo.com

goowy, www.goowy.com

Google Talk (from within Gmail), mail.google.com

Library Success Wiki, Online Reference entry, www.libsuccess.org/index.php?title=Online_Reference

iTunes, www.apple.com/itunes

The Podcasters Wiki, www.podcasterswiki.com

Audacity, audacity.sourceforge.net

Lansing Public Library, www.lansing.lib.il.us

MySpace, www.myspace.com

"Freedom Teen Zone" MySpace profile, www.myspace.com/freedomteenzone

"The Loft @ ImaginOn" MySpace profile, www.myspace.com/libraryloft

Hennepin County Library MySpace profile, www.myspace.com/hennepincountylibrary

Friendster, www.friendster.com

Flickr, www.flickr.com

Bloomington Public Library Flickr page, www.flickr.com/photos/bloomingtonlibrary

"Libraries and Librarians" Flickr group, www.flickr.com/groups/librariesandlibrarians

"Librarian Trading Cards" Flickr group, www.flickr.com/groups/librariancards

Librarian Trading Cards blog, librariantradingcards.blogspot.com

Appendix C:
References and
Other Resources

The following resources list, although not comprehensive, contains material that may answer additional questions you might have on Library 2.0 or on additional topics not fully covered in this book.

Abram, Stephen. "Web 2.0—Huh?! Library 2.0, Librarian 2.0." *Information Outlook* (December 1, 2005): 44–46.

Anderson, Chris. *The Long Tail: Why the Future of Business Is Selling Less of More.* New York: Hyperion, 2006.

Beitler, Michael. *Strategic Organizational Change: A Practitioner's Guide for Managers and Consultants.* Greensboro, NC: Practitioner Press International, 2001.

Breeding, Marshall. "Designing Sites to Distribute Content via Various Mechanisms." *Computers in Libraries* (January 1, 2006): 20–23.

Breeding, Marshall. "Web 2.0? Let's Get to Web 1.0 First." *Computers in Libraries* (May 1, 2006): 30–33.

Cameron, Esther and Mike Green. *Making Sense of Change Management: A Complete Guide to the Models, Tools & Techniques of Organizational Change.* Sterling, VA: Kogan, 2004.

Chad, Ken and Paul Miller. "Do Libraries Matter? The Rise of Library 2.0." November 2005. www.talis.com/downloads/white_papers/Do LibrariesMatter.pdf.

Clumpner, Krista E. "Delivering Access to Library Materials and Services: Our Recipe for Success." *Computers in Libraries* (October 1, 2004): 6-8, 56.

Cohen, Alex. "Libraries, Knowledge Management, and Communities of Practice." *Information Outlook* (January 1, 2006): 34–37.

Cox, Christopher. "Brick and Click Libraries Symposium." *Library Hi Tech News* (December 1, 2005): 7–8.

Crawford, Walt. "Library 2.0 and 'Library 2.0'." *Cites & Insights* 6:2 (Midwinter 2006). cites.boisestate.edu/civ6i2.pdf.

Friedman, Thomas L. *The World Is Flat: A Brief History of the Twenty-First Century*. New York: Farrar, Straus and Giroux, 2006.

Gordon, Rachel Singer and Michael Stephens. "Welcome to Our World!" *Computers in Libraries* (January 1, 2006): 40–41.

Hiatt, Jeffrey M. Hiatt and Timothy J. Creasey. *Change Management*. Loveland, CO: Prosci Research, 2003.

Johnson, Steven. "Web 2.0 Arrives." *Discover* (October 1, 2005): 20–21.

Levine, Rick, Christopher Locke, Doc Searls, and David Weinberger. *The Cluetrain Manifesto: The End of Business as Usual*. Cambridge, MA: Perseus Books, 2000.

"Libraries urged to embrace Web 2.0." *Information World Review* (January 1, 2006): 1.

Managing Change and Transition. Boston, MA: Harvard Business School Press, 2003.

Miller, Paul. "Library 2.0: The Challenge of Disruptive Innovation." February 2006. www.talis.com/resources/documents/447_Library_2_prf1.pdf.

Miller, Paul. "Web 2.0: Building the New Library." *Ariadne* 45

(October 30, 2005). www.ariadne.ac.uk/issue45/miller/intro.html.

Morville, Peter. *Ambient Findability*. Sebastopol, CA: O'Reilly, 2005.

Nelson, Sandra. *The New Planning For Results: A Streamlined Approach*. Chicago: ALA, 2001.

Nesting, Vicki. "WebJunction Launched to Help Public Libraries Make the Most of Technology." *Public Libraries* (November 1, 2003): 394.

Notess, Greg R. "The Terrible Twos: Web 2.0, Library 2.0, and More." *ONLINE* (May 1, 2006): 40–42.

OCLC. *Perceptions of Libraries and Information Resources*, Dublin, OH: OCLC, 2005.

Roush, Wade. 2005. "Social Machines." *Technology Review* (August 1, 2005): 44–53.

Schonfeld, Erick. "Web 2.0 Around the World." *Business 2.0* (August 1, 2006): 105.

Scoble, Robert and Shel Israel. *Naked Conversations: How Blogs are Changing the Way Businesses Talk with Customers*. Hoboken, NJ: John Wiley, 2006.

Shiu, Eulynn and Amanda Lenhart. "How Americans Use Instant Messaging." *PEW Report* (August 31, 2004). www.pewinternet.org/PPF/r/133/report_display.asp.

Stephens, Michael. "Technoplans vs. Technolust." *Library Journal* (November 1, 2004). www.libraryjournal.com/article/CA474999.html.

Stephens, Michael and Aaron Schmidt. "IM Me." *Library Journal* (April 1, 2005). www.libraryjournal.com/article/CA512192.html.

Tebbutt, David. "Is All the Talk of Web 2.0 Just a Lot of Codswallop?" *Information World Review* (February 1, 2006): 9.

Webster, Peter. "Interconnected and Innovative Libraries: Factors Tying Libraries More Closely Together." *Library Trends* 54:3 (January 1, 2006): 382–393.

SUGGESTED MAGAZINES

Business 2.0., Business 2.0 Media Inc.

Business Week, McGraw-Hill

Computers in Libraries, Information Today, Inc.

Economist, Economist Newspaper Limited

Technology Review, MIT

Wired, Wired USA

ADDITIONAL WEB RESOURCES

An always-updated OPML file that you can plug in to your RSS reader is available at www.librarychange.com

ALA TechSource Blog, www.techsource.ala.org/blog

Blyberg.net, www.blyberg.net

Church of the Customer, blogs.bnet.com/church

Cites & Insights, www.cical.info

The Cluetrain Manifesto, www.cluetrain.com

David Lee King, www.davidleeking.com

Free Range Librarian, www.freerangelibrarian.com

Information Wants To Be Free, meredith.wolfwater.com

Librarian 1.5, lib1point5.wordpress.com

Library 2.0 Reading List, www.squidoo.com/library20

Library Stuff, www.librarystuff.net

Open Stacks, www.openstacks.net/os

Peter Morville's Findability, www.findability.org

Pew Internet & American Life Project, www.pewinternet.org

Read/Write Web, www.readwriteweb.com

SirsiDynix Institute, www.sirsidynixinstitute.com

Stephen's Lighthouse, stephenslighthouse.sirsi.com

Talking with Talis, talk.talis.com

Tame the Web, www.tametheweb.com

TechCrunch, www.techcrunch.com

Technology Review, www.technologyreview.com

The Shifted Librarian, www.theshiftedlibrarian.com

Web 2.0 Explorer, blogs.zdnet.com/web2explorer

About the Authors

Michael E. Casey is the division director of technology services for the Gwinnett County Public Library in Lawrenceville, GA. Michael was a branch manager prior to moving into his current position, and participated in the construction of the library's Dacula branch. He is also the author of the blog LibraryCrunch (www.librarycrunch.com). Michael has given numerous presentations on Library 2.0, and has participated in several Web seminars and podcasts on the topic. Michael holds an MA in political science from Penn State, an MLS from Southern Connecticut State, and a BA in political science and history from Duquesne University. Originally from Pennsylvania, Michael now resides in Georgia with his family.

Laura C. Savastinuk is an assistant branch manager with the Gwinnett County Public Library in Lawrenceville, GA. She holds an MSLIS from the University of Illinois at Urbana-Champaign. She also earned a BS in history, technology, and society from the Georgia Institute of Technology. Laura resides in Georgia with her husband, Paul.

Index

computer literacy of, 24
drive-arounds, 30
events in the library, 136–137
feasibility studies and, 50
feedback from, 137
governing board responsibility to,
    110
Library 2.0 and, 114–115
library ownership and, 23
trends within, 105
competition
    sharing ideas, 131
    for user time, 4–5
    visits to, 55, 128
competitors, 34–35
computer literacy, 24
computers in libraries, 104–105, 135
credibility, leadership and, 80
crisis management, 49
customer comment cards, 62
customer service, 120
customers. *see also* users
    changing expectations, 4
    communication with, 75
    content added by, 59
    content created by, 136
    involvement of, 123–128
    participation by, 74, 136
    reactions to change, 108–109
customization, 63, 68, *69*

D

Dallas Public Library, 26–27
Daly, James, 2
Darien (CT) Library, 62, 71, *72*
data collection, 55
decision making, participatory,
    47–49

Deleting Online Predators Act
    (DOPA, H.R. 5319), 101
demographics
    changes in, 2, 30
    community, 29–30
    of users, 23–25
departments, library, 78–81, 112
DeWolfe, Chris, 95
digital rights management (DRM),
    17
digital video recorders, 95
Directors, open letter to, 40–44
Dougherty, Dale, 74
downloads, libraries and, 17
downtime, efficiency and, 4
drive-arounds, 30, 55
Drupal, 68, 83, 84
DVD collections, 65

E

e-mail, 136
eBay, 64, 74
efficiency, downtime and, 4
electronic games, 34
Ellsworth Public Library, 26
emerging technology teams,
    129–131
enthusiasm, harnessing of, 41
events, 84

F

Facebook, 90, 97
facilities, physical layout, 16
FactCheck.org, 60
Farkas, Meredith, 89–90
feasibility studies, 49–50, 55–56
Federal Trade Commission, 96

More Great Books from Information Today, Inc.

Social Software in Libraries
Building Collaboration, Communication, and Community Online

By Meredith G. Farkas

This guide provides librarians with the information and skills necessary to implement the most popular and effective social software technologies: blogs, RSS, wikis, social networking software, screencasting, photo-sharing, podcasting, instant messaging, gaming, and more. Success stories and interviews highlight these tools' ease-of-use—and tremendous impact. Novice readers will find ample descriptions and advice on using each technology, while veteran users of social software will discover new applications and approaches. Supported by the author's Web page.

344 pp/softbound/ISBN 978-1-57387-275-1 $39.50

The Thriving Library
Successful Strategies for Challenging Times

By Marylaine Block

Here is a highly readable guide to strategies and projects that have helped more than 100 public libraries gain community support and funding during challenging times. Marylaine Block integrates survey responses from innovative library directors with her research, analysis, and extended interviews to showcase hundreds of winning programs and services. The strategies explored include youth services, the library as place, partnerships, marketing, stressing the economic value, Library 2.0, outreach, and helping the community achieve its aspirations.

352 pp/softbound/ISBN 978-1-57387-277-5 $39.50

Blogging & RSS
A Librarian's Guide

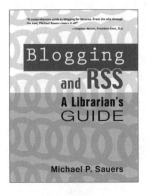

By Michael P. Sauers

Author, Internet trainer, and blogger Michael P. Sauers, MLS, shows how blogging and RSS technology can be easily and effectively used in the context of a library community. Sauers showcases interesting and useful blogs, shares insights from librarian bloggers, and offers step-by-step instructions for creating, publishing, and syndicating a blog using free Web-based services, software, RSS feeds, and aggregators.

288 pp/softbound/ISBN 978-1-57387-268-3 $29.50

The NextGen Librarian's Survival Guide

By Rachel Singer Gordon

This unique resource addresses the specific needs of GenXers and Millenials as they work to define themselves as information professionals. The book focuses on how NextGens can move their careers forward and positively impact the profession. Library career guru Rachel Singer Gordon provides timely advice along with tips and insights from dozens of librarians on issues ranging from image to stereotypes, to surviving library school and entry-level positions, to working with older colleagues.

224 pp/softbound/ISBN 978-1-57387-256-0 $29.50